Following God

Living

GOD'S WILL

READING AND APPLYING GOD'S SIGNS FOR YOUR LIFE

What Christian Leaders Are Saying about *Living God's Will* . . .

You wont regret the time you spend reading Eddie Rasnake's book. I count it a privilege to know him personally and work with him. His book will help you read the signposts of decisions correctly and properly.

Dr. Spiros Zodhiates, Author
President, AMG International

As I travel around our world, I find Christians everywhere asking the all-important question, "What is God's will?" Eddie Rasnake's book provides sound scriptural direction in helping us find the answer to that question. I highly recommend it.

Dr. Bill Bright, Founder and President
Campus Crusade for Christ

Eddie Rasnake has given us clarity and insight along with solid scriptural examples of how God leads people as we enter the twenty-first century. His book has already been helpful to me personally, and I expect the same result in the lives of multitudes.

Dan Hayes, Author
Director, National Collegiate Prayer Alliance

As a minister for more than thirty years, I have often sought to give counsel about God's will. I have never found a book as clear, concise, and simple as Eddie Rasnake's book. It was a blessing to me to read it, and I recommend it to all.

Dr. Robert C. Burch, Senior Pastor
Calvary Baptist Church
Knoxville, Tennessee

Throughout my ministry of forty-one years, I have never read anything more fresh and enlightening than this book of knowing and living the will of God.

Rev. Bill Stafford, Evangelist
Director, International Congress on Revival

Fresh, original, imaginative—and biblical—were the words that came to mind as I read [this book]. Easy reading makes the principles accessible even to the newest Christian.

Ron Dunn, Author, Conference Speaker
Director, LifeStyle Ministries

I highly recommend this book not only to the new believer struggling with the topic for the first time, but also to the older saint who would like a fresh look at how to discover God's will. Eddie has a non-threatening way of saying hard things, and he deftly and practically presents biblical truth in a palatable, memorable style. It is a refreshing look at a well-worn subject.

Jan Silvious, Author
Christian Radio Personality

GOD'S WILL

READING AND APPLYING GOD'S SIGNS
FOR YOUR LIFE

A BIBLE STUDY BY
EDDIE RASNAKE

AMG *Publishers*
Chattanooga, TN 37422

Following God

LIVING GOD'S WILL: READING AND APPLYING GOD'S SIGNS FOR YOUR LIFE

ISBN 10: 0-89957-309-6
ISBN 13: 978-0-89957-309-0

Cover design by Phillip Rodgers
Text editing and page layout by Rick Steele

Printed in Canada
13 12 11 10 09 08 –T– 12 11 10 9 8 7

This book is dedicated to the late Ron Dunn.

From my earliest days in the faith, Ron has always been a great encouragement and example to me and so many others. Heaven's gain is our loss.

"Remember those who led you, who spoke the word of God to you; and considering the results of their conduct, imitate their faith" Hebrews 13:7.

Acknowledgments

This work goes forth to those who have encouraged us in the publication of the first six books in this series: *Life Principles from the Old Testament, Life Principles from the Kings of the Old Testament, Life Principles from the Women of the Bible, Life Principles from the Prophets of the Old Testament, Life Principles from the New Testament Men of Faith,* and *Life Principles for Worship from the Tabernacle.* This series has been a labor of love, and through our study we have made friends with many saints of days gone by. We look forward to getting to know them even better in heaven. We are especially grateful to those who have walked through many of these studies with us and have been a continual source of encouragement as the writing of new studies progresses. Thanks to the folks at AMG, especially Warren Baker and Rick Steele, Trevor Overcash and Dale Anderson, and to Phillip Rodgers. Most of all, we remain grateful to the Lord Jesus, who continues to teach us and lead us in what it means to follow Him with a whole heart.

THE AUTHORS OF
THE
FOLLOWING GOD SERIES

About the Author

Eddie Rasnake met Christ in 1976 as a freshman in college. He graduated with honors from East Tennessee State University in 1980. He and his wife, Michele, served for nearly seven years on the staff of Campus Crusade for Christ. Their first assignment was the University of Virginia, and while there they also started a Campus Crusade ministry at James Madison University. Eddie then served four years as campus director of the Campus Crusade ministry at the University of Tennessee. In 1989, Eddie left Campus Crusade to join Wayne Barber at Woodland Park Baptist Church as the Associate Pastor of Discipleship and Training. He has been ministering in Eastern Europe in the role of equipping local believers for more than a decade and has published materials in Albanian, Greek, Italian, Romanian, and Russian. Eddie serves on the boards of directors of the Center for Christian Leadership in Tirana, Albania, and the Bible Training Center in Eleuthera, Bahamas. He also serves as chaplain for the Chattanooga Lookouts (Cincinnati Reds AA affiliate) baseball team. Eddie and his wife Michele live in Chattanooga, Tennessee with their four children.

About the Following God Series

Three authors and fellow ministers, Wayne Barber, Eddie Rasnake, and Rick Shepherd, teamed up in 1998 to write a character-based Bible study for AMG Publishers. Their collaboration developed into the title, *Life Principles from the Old Testament*. Since 1998 these same authors and AMG Publishers have produced four more character-based studies—each consisting of twelve lessons geared around a five-day study of a particular Bible personality. More studies of this type are in the works. Two unique titles were added to the series in 2001: *Life Principles for Worship from the Tabernacle* and *Living God's Will*. These titles are unique in that they are the first Following God studies that are topically-based rather than character-based. However, the interactive study format that readers have come to love remains constant in both new titles. *Living God's Will* also marks the first Following God title to be written by only one author, Eddie Rasnake. As new titles are being planned, our focus remains the same: to provide excellent Bible study materials that point people to God's Word in ways that allow them to apply truths to their own lives. More information on this groundbreaking series can be found on the following web pages:

www.followingGod.com
www.amgpublishers.com

Preface

Do you want to know what God's will for your life is? **HE WANTS YOU TO KNOW EVEN MORE!!** Discerning His will is not a game of hide-and-seek. It is not some kind of cosmic easter egg hunt where God camouflages His will and we have to try and find where it is hidden. God never hides His will. So why do we struggle with knowing what God's will is?

One of the reasons I felt this book needed to be written, was the fact that so many Christians I meet all over the world struggle with this same issue on a fundamental level. We need to know how God speaks, and we need to know how to hear what He is saying. We need to know how God speaks His will to us through the fundamental aspects of a relationship with Him—prayer, faith, waiting, surrender, studying the Scriptures, etc. How God speaks and how we hear Him are not separate issues from a daily walk with Christ; they are part of the whole.

As I talk with people everywhere—in America, in Eastern Europe, in the Caribbean, wherever—I find that most Christians struggle with God's will at one common point. More of a problem than our finding God's will is our settling that God's will is what we want. I have a will also. And when God's will and my will don't match, a decision must be made. I must answer the question: "Who is Lord of this area of my life?" It doesn't matter what I sing, what I profess, or what I believe intellectually. If I choose my will over God's in any particular area, then Christ is not Lord in that area—self is. What I have seen as I counsel Christians everywhere is that choosing to do God's will trips people up far more frequently than an inability to find it, and that is where I struggle also. What about you?

It is my conviction that the road to God's will is well-marked with signposts to direct us. But we have to spot these signposts, interpret what they mean, and then choose to follow them. Come join me in this journey of finding and living God's will!

Eddie Rasnake

EDDIE RASNAKE

Table of Contents

BEGINNING THE PROCESS: Recognizing Signposts

Julie tossed nervously in her bed, unable to sleep. Her mind raced as she tried to process her circumstances. Tonight as they sat in the dorm lobby talking, Bill had brought up the subject of marriage again. Their relationship is moving so fast, yet she feels she is in love with him. Maybe he *is* the one. But she just isn't sure. "What should I do, Lord?" she implores in prayer.

Sam nervously broke the lead of his pencil as he scratched meaninglessly at the project he was on which he was working. He couldn't seem to focus on the work. His mind kept leaping back to the decision he had to make. The job offer seemed too good to be true; a $10,000 raise, his own secretary, a company car, and a job he felt he could really sink his teeth into. But it would require moving halfway across the state, leaving all their friends, their family and their church. In addition it would uproot the kids from school, and their son, Steve, had just been accepted on the varsity football team. "What should I do, Lord?" Sam pleaded in an exasperated tone.

Danny's stomach churned in knots as he ineptly played with the food on his plate. He had no appetite for it even though Mom had fixed his favorite dinner. Graduation was only three weeks away and he still had no idea what he was going to do this summer, let alone the rest of his life. Should he go on to graduate school and get a master's degree, or should he accept his dad's offer and take a position in the family business? Deep in his heart he really wanted to join his friend Dave and do missions work in South America, but he knew there was no way his parents would go for that. Under his breath he mouthed the words in a heartfelt cry: "What should I do, Lord?"

"What should I do, Lord?" Have you ever found yourself praying that prayer? If you are like me, it has shown up in your silent conversations more than once. Often, we quietly wish God would just write His will in big letters across the sky or speak to us audibly. Perhaps like me, you are pretty leery of those who say "God told me. . ." but at the same time you wish He also would "tell" you.

We grapple with God's will because, first of all, we believe He knows what is best. But deeper than that, in our heart of hearts we don't want to suffer the consequences of making a wrong decision, so we want God to make the decision for us. He doesn't always make decisions for us as neatly as we'd like. Yet He does want to lead us, and contrary to the teaching of some, what we decide does make a difference.

The Scriptures are not silent about God's will. In fact, the subject comes up quite often. The problem we sometimes have in discerning God's will is not that He isn't revealing His will like in times past. It seems to me the problem is that we have lost sight of how God communicates, and we aren't looking for answers in the right places. In the pages ahead you'll find out where those right places are. This book doesn't offer "ivory tower" ideologies but practical, usable principles distilled from God's Word and explained on a grass-roots level. Don't worry, "The cookies are on the bottom shelf."

The pursuit of God's guidance is not some kind of spiritual Easter-egg hunt where God disguises His will and says, "Find it if you can." It is my conviction that the road to God's will is well marked with signposts to direct us. But we have to spot those signposts, interpret what they mean, and then choose to follow them.

The crucial first step in this process of discerning the will of God is **observation** (spotting the signposts). If we do not see the signposts God places before us, if we are not looking for them, we cannot expect to find God's will. But the process doesn't end there.

We may observe these signposts, but if our senses are not trained to **interpret** them (rightly understand what they mean), they are of no more benefit to us than Braille to someone who isn't blind. Even if we do observe the signposts and accurately interpret them, they will not help us until we *apply* them (obey what they say).

Let me give you a good parallel: A stop sign doesn't protect you from wrecking your car if you don't stop at it. And to stop at it, you must first see it. Then you must understand what the sign says, and then you must act on it. God's signposts work the same way. The process breaks down if we omit any one of these parts.

Observation, interpretation, and application are a part of communication on any level. If these steps for seeking God's will sound like the process of Bible study to you, it isn't by accident. The Bible is God's recorded will, and—equally important to our process—it is God's communication to us. In the pages ahead you will learn how to connect with God in his communication process, how to interpret what He says, and, through practical application questions, how to evaluate your situation and act on God's will. I've paved the road for you but you'll have to drive the vehicle.

Before we start identifying these signposts of God's will, we must consider some important preliminaries: We need to get God's perspective—we need to think rightly about His will.

What God's Will Is Like

Unfortunately, most of us operate from a woefully deficient picture of God and how He views us. Instead of seeing Him as the Good Shepherd and Loving Father, we tend to react toward Him as if He were the proverbial "gray-headed old man with a stick." We imagine Him looking out over the battlements of heaven for people who are having fun just so He can whack them and tell them to "cut it out!"

As author and speaker Dan Hayes puts it, often we are guilty of believing that to be in God's will means "hopping the first boat to Borneo and spending the rest of the our life swabbing sores in some native hut." But I wonder how many of us, deep down, under our whitewashed veneer of spirituality, really believe God's will for our lives is good—even if we don't go to Borneo? I am reminded of the old Quaker who in a moment of honesty with God said, "I'm not surprised You don't have any more friends than You do because of the way You treat the ones You have."

The Scriptures, however, paint a very different picture of God and His will. He is *the Father of mercies, and the God of all comfort"* (2 Corinthians 1:3), the Good Shepherd who lays down His life for His sheep (John 10:11), the Sovereign God who loves us so much He calls us His children (1 John 3:1), the Father who gives only good gifts (James 1:17)—and the list goes on and on. God's desire for us is not to make us miserable but to make our lives meaningful and to make us more like Himself.

In Romans 12:2 we see a clear description of God's will: *"that which is good, and acceptable, and perfect."* Think about that. God's will for you really is good! His will is acceptable (the Greek word translated "acceptable"means "well-pleasing," "agreeable"), and it is perfect (having the idea of "that which meets the need of the person"). God's will for you and me is all this and more.

Let's be honest with each other. Haven't you sometimes struggled with wanting to choose your own will over God's? I have. Just think how much it would help us in these situations if we really understood that His will, His specific desire for us in that circumstance, was good, acceptable, and perfect. Right now you may be seeking God's will. What a comfort to know with certainty that His will is better for you than your own will is!

WHY WE NEED GOD'S WILL

Have you ever taken the time to ask yourself, "*Why* do I need to know God's will?" Probably not. That's not the kind of question a Christian is supposed to ask, but being able to answer it is of real benefit. It is the "whys" that enable us consistently to do the "hows." Perhaps the best single answer to the "why" question is found in Ephesians 5:15–17 where we are exhorted: "*Be careful how you walk, not as unwise men, but as wise, making the most of your time, because the days are evil. So then do not be foolish, but understand what the will of the Lord is.*"

The thing that differentiates the wise man from the foolish is that the wise man "understands God's will." It is impossible for us to make the most of our time in these evil days without knowing God's will for us. Based on this we can safely say that God wills that we know His will.

In Colossians 1:9 the apostle Paul relates this same truth in a slightly different way. He prays that the Colossian believers would be "*filled with the knowledge of His will in all spiritual wisdom and understanding.*"

In verse 10 he gives the reason for this prayer: "*so that you may walk in a manner worthy of the Lord, to please Him in all respects.*" You see, it is impossible to walk worthy of the Lord or to please the Lord apart from discerning and doing His will.

THE PROMISE OF GOD'S WILL

We know we need God's will, but often I think we end up feeling like a donkey chasing a carrot on a stick: No matter how hard we try, we can't seem to catch it. The truth is, if we are seeking God's will and not finding it, the problem is likely on our end. Our Lord promises: "*If any of you lacks wisdom, let him ask of God who gives to all men generously and without reproach*" (James 1:5).

As you travel down the road toward God's will, pay special attention to the common mistakes people make, and you will avoid many a pitfall. This book offers no promise of divine skywriting or voices from the beyond, but if you follow God's principles, you *will* find His will. And in the process, you will learn more about how He communicates. I'll be honest with you. There are really only two reasons I wrote this book:

First: I know what it feels like to grapple with God's will, and I want to help you find it.

Second: If I can walk you through the process in a practical way and help you succeed in hearing what God is saying to you now, I also will have moved you further down the road toward the future. Then the next time you need to know God's leading, the process will be easier for you. I don't want you just to know God's will; I want you to know also how to follow Him as a way of life, hearing all that He has to say to you.

THE BINARY TRAP

One of the most common things that trip us up in the process of discerning God's direction is what I call the "Binary Trap." Let me explain what I mean by that. When it comes to decision making, all too often we reduce the determination to only two options: an either-or, "binary" choice. That may not sound like any big deal, but slipping into this mode can send us speeding down the wrong road. The problem is, if we've come up with the options ourselves, both may be wrong.

As a sophomore in college I grappled with a decision that was important to me. I'd become a Christian as a freshman at a moderately-sized state school in the South, and now as I grew in my relationship with Christ, I wondered if it might be better to transfer to a Christian college where I could deepen my knowledge of the Scriptures. I also played soccer, and at the particular Christian college that interested me, the level of coaching and competition would be much greater than where I was. On the other hand, if I stayed, I could continue to reach out in ministry to those around me.

My approach to solving this decision-making dilemma was to ask God, "Should I stay at the secular school or transfer to the Christian school?" At face value this may seem fine, but I had already made a crucial mistake. I had limited myself to only two options: an either-or decision. While this type of decision may be easier to make than one with many options, I hadn't considered the possibility that neither option would be God's way of solving my problem. As a result, the decision became far more involved and emotional than it really needed to be.

After several weeks of agonizing and plenty of Alka-Seltzers, I finally sat down and tried to identify exactly what needs I was trying to meet. In this case, I sensed a need for a deeper knowledge of the Scriptures, and I desired to be where I could grow in my soccer skills and determine how far I could go with them. No problem there. Nothing is wrong with either of those desires. So the two primary relevant factors were:

1. Developing biblically
2. Developing my soccer skills

If that were you, what would you decide? Like me, faced with those two objectives and limited to those two options, you probably would decide to transfer to the Christian school. In this case, however, that wasn't God's will. I believe that if I had followed through and changed schools, I would have forfeited forever some of the most significant opportunities to minister that I had in my young Christian life. Although attending this particular Christian college would have deepened my knowledge of God's Word, I believe in some ways it would have hindered my applying it. The incredible opportunities to minister on a secular college campus are unparalleled in almost every other segment of our society, and God blessed me enormously as I pursued them.

So how did I make the decision? Through the counsel of a good friend, God showed me the binary trap into which I had placed myself, and I finally prayed, "Would another option meet these objectives better?"

How liberating that prayer was. Before very long I found out about a summer option that radically changed the whole process. My discipler shared with me about the Institute of Biblical Studies, a sort of summer-school seminary where I could deepen my knowledge of both the Old and New Testaments and of basic biblical doctrines. This particular summer, the Athletes in Action soccer team, a Christian post-college competition group, happened to be working out at the same location. I asked for and was given permission to work out with them for the summer.

I have no doubt that was God's will. This third option provided the benefits of a Christian college and then some, without requiring me to forfeit the ministry I had at a secular school. But finding it required that I break out of the binary trap.

So what got me into the binary trap? Three things, primarily. First, I hadn't prayed sufficiently. Second, I had not adequately counted the cost. Third, I hadn't solicited the counsel from others. Once I did those three things I was able to break free and find God's will.

How about you? Have you slipped into a binary trap? I realize sometimes that trap seems comfortable. For example, when a man asks a woman to marry him, isn't the decision really a yes or no decision? **No, it isn't!** That is why the binary trap is so sneaky. When a man asks a woman to marry him, that woman has at least three options: **(1)** Say yes and marry him; **(2)** say no and break up; **(3)** say wait, I'm not ready for this decision yet. Perhaps the woman doesn't know the man enough, or there are uncertainties about their future, or whatever. Don't let someone else force you into a binary trap.

A book on the will of God written during the '70's suggested that the Lord really doesn't care whether I have pancakes or waffles for breakfast. As long as my decision doesn't violate some clear directive of Scripture, it really doesn't matter what I decide. While at a glance this may appear logical, it reduces decisions to a binary level. Although God may not have a preference in my choosing waffles or pancakes, He may prefer neither of the options I am offering Him.

Instead, He may prefer that I eat something more nutritious. You see, our real need isn't simply God's *will* in a particular decision; we need His *wisdom* as well.

We need His perspective and His eternal value system to filter through our decisions. This book isn't simply to help you discover the decision God has already made for you; it is also to help you understand the principles of His Word and be able to follow them in other decisions He calls you to make.

Although binary reasoning may be appropriate in some circumstances, those situations are a lot more rare than we think. If you struggle with binary reasoning, there is hope for you. You can find the freedom and ability to discover God's will, even if it isn't one of your two choices. Remember, God wants you to know His will even more than you do, and He will show it to you. You just have to learn how to hear what He is saying. And you will! That's what this book is all about.

MAKING IT PERSONAL

Why did you buy this book? Perhaps you picked it up simply to learn principles about God's will for your own interest and growth. Or more likely, you need to know God's will in your present circumstances. Why not take a few minutes now and identify a specific area that is troubling you? Then as you work through the principles in the pages ahead, you can focus them on something particular and apply the truths to your immediate need.

Don't worry if your first pass is a little sketchy; you will refine your skill as you work through the process.

The Decision to Be Made (be as specific as possible)

_____

_____

_____

_____

_____

_____

_____

_____

_____

_____

Options Available to Me:

#1

_____

_____

_____

_____

_____

_____

#2

_____

_____

_____

_____

_____

_____

#3

_____

_____

_____

_____

_____

_____

THE YIELD SIGN:
Settling the Lordship Question

Beth tossed restlessly as the bed sheets tangled in knots of disarray. The glow of her digital clock glared the lateness of the hour, yet sleep was elusive. Her mind replayed the day's events like a videocassette. She had been excited when Sara called months earlier and asked her to be a bridesmaid. They had been roommates in college and even though their paths hadn't crossed much lately, it was still a special relationship. Now though, she wished she had never come to this wedding. Oh, it was great to see the old friends and catch up, but she'd never before felt so conspicuously single. It seemed all her college chums were married and starting families.

"Come on, Beth, catch the bouquet!" they cheered as if trying to will her a mate. She hadn't really minded her friends' probing inquiry, "How's your love life?" at the time, but now her nerves pounded with the raw emotion of reality.

She wasn't getting any younger. The biological time clock was ticking, especially if she wanted children. In a few months I'll be thirty, she thought. Gee, that sounds scary. Maybe I'm just too particular. Maybe "Mr. Right" doesn't exist. Maybe it's time to start looking for "Mr. Okay." Bob certainly fits that bill.

"Lord, I want to be married. . . . I'm tired of being single."

—"Beth"

They had met at their Atlanta-based law office's Christmas party a year earlier and had dated pretty steadily ever since. *He's reasonably good looking,* she mused, checking off his credentials. *He holds a good position in the firm's bankruptcy section...probably be a junior partner in a few years.*

Sure, he didn't really have the same heart for God as she did, but he had started going to church with her sometimes, and lately he had been bringing up the subject of marriage. He seemed to want to settle down.

"Maybe that would mean less time running around and more time for God. Lord, I know he'll come to share my commitment to You," Beth exclaimed. She mouthed the words intensely as if trying to convince herself as much as God. "Lord, I want to be married. . . . I'm tired of being single," she implored as she finally drifted off to sleep.

Several weeks later Bob surprised Beth with an engagement ring. In the excitement of the moment she silently prayed, "Lord, please bless our marriage." Had Beth found God's will, or had she simply decided what she wanted it to be?

YIELD SIGN

Day One

THE LORDSHIP QUESTION

WHAT DOES IT MEAN TO "YIELD"?

Perhaps the most important signpost on the way to God's will is the one which reads **YIELD.** One of the reasons why people are not able to find God's will is because they have an attitude that suggests, *"Lord, show me what You want me to do so I can decide if I want to do it."* This attitude subtly communicates a perspective of our wanting the final say in the decision instead of leaving it to the Lord, and it suggests our mistrust of God's intent for us.

📖 Look at Romans 12:2. How does Paul describe God's will in this verse?

Good, acceptable and perfect

_____

_____

> "...That you may prove what the will of God is, that which is good and acceptable and perfect."
>
> Romans 12:2

In Romans 12:2 we see a clear description of God's will: *"that which is good and acceptable and perfect."* Think about that. God's will for you personally really is *"good"*! His will is *"acceptable"* (the Greek word means "well-pleasing, agreeable"), and it is *"perfect"* (having the idea of "that which meets the need of the person"). God's will for you and me is all these things and more.

Let's be honest with each other. Haven't you sometimes struggled with wanting to choose your own will over God's? I have. Just think how much it would help us in these situations if we really understood that His will, His specific desire for us in that circumstance, is good, acceptable, and perfect. Right now you may be seeking God's will. What a comfort to know with certainty that His will is better for you than your own will is!

Had Beth found God's will, or had she simply decided what she wanted it to be?

Often we doubt the words of Romans 12:2 that say God's will really is good. We want the right to put a "presidential veto" on anything that doesn't seem good to us or on anything that we don't want to do. But God is not the U.S. Congress, and He will not be mocked.

God is not going to show us His will until we first settle in our hearts that we are willing to do **whatever He says.** God's will is not a choice to be made, but a command to be followed. Unless we are submitted to Him, He isn't going to waste His breath giving us orders. But, as peerless theologian Lewis Sperry Chafer wrote in his book, *He That Is Spiritual* (Zondervan, 1918): "God is able to speak loud enough to make a **willing** soul hear" (emphasis mine).

Until we reach the point of yielding to God and trusting Him with each area of our lives, we will be like the doubting man of James chapter 1—driven and tossed by the winds as a wave of the sea. James' verdict: "*Let not that man expect that he will receive anything from the Lord, being a double-minded man* [lit. 'two-souled,' a fence straddler], *unstable in all his ways*" (1:7–8).

📖 Now look at Romans 12:1–2. What prerequisites do you see there for finding the *"good acceptable and perfect"* will of God?

Surrender to Him - always!

If we want to find that good, acceptable, and perfect will of God that Romans 12:2 speaks of, we must first settle the decision Romans 12:1 calls for: "*I urge you therefore, brethren, by the mercies of God, to present your bodies a living and holy sacrifice, acceptable to God, which is your spiritual service of worship.*"

Although I realize it sounds a bit paradoxical that the first step to finding God's will is yielding ourselves to it. God wants us to answer yes, and then He will tell us what the question is. We all realize that Jesus Christ is Lord. What this passage shows is the need for us to let the Lord Jesus Christ be Lord in us. Had Beth done that in her decision?

WHAT DOES IT MEAN FOR JESUS TO BE LORD?

We often see the lordship of Christ over our lives as being similar to the role of the king or queen in a "constitutional monarchy." The most familiar example of a constitutional monarchy is the nation of Great Britain, which is presided over by a reigning monarch; yet Parliament, not the king or queen, makes the rules and decisions. Today, out of deference to the monarch, a solid black line for the queen's signature appears in the lower right hand corner at the end of every bill Parliament passes. Upon passage, the bill is sent to Buckingham Palace for the Queen's

YIELD SIGN

Day Two

THE LORDSHIP QUESTION

consideration, and by signing on the provided space, she gives her approval of the newly-enacted law. Nevertheless, the interesting thing about this is that even if she refuses to sign the bill, it still becomes law. Her lordship or sovereignty over the country is merely symbolic—the Prime Minister and Parliament actually "run the country."

All too often we try to set up our lives as constitutional monarchies. We have a position and place for an absolute monarch (Jesus Christ), yet we make all the decisions and then ask the Lord to approve our plans. The convicting reality I see, as I seek to follow the Lord, is that Christianity is not a constitutional monarchy. God does not want to approve *my* plans; He wants my approval of *His* plans, and He wants me to submit to them. That is what it means for Christ to be Lord. Anything less is not true biblical Christianity.

📖 Look at the verses listed below and summarize in your own words their message.

Luke 6:46

Why do we not listen

Matthew 21:28–32

He is not the God of the dead but of the living

John 7:17

Belief in the one whom God has sent

The point in each of these passages is that following Jesus as Lord is not lip-service. It is not enough for us to simply say Jesus is Lord—our surrender to Him should be seen in our actions and choices. As Jesus put it, *"Why do you call Me, 'Lord, Lord,' and do not do what I say?"* (Luke 6:46). That same idea is seen in Jesus' parable in Matthew 21. A key point to consider is this one put forward in John 7:17, namely, that our surrender to God affects our ability to hear Him. When we are surrendered, we are able to discern which options are from God and which are not.

YIELD SIGN

Day Three

THE LORDSHIP QUESTION

BARRIERS TO OBEYING THE YIELD SIGN

The two most devious and dangerous lures that keep us from obeying God's **YIELD** sign are **pride** and **self-centeredness**. Both are satanic influences that are subtle in their approach and sneaky in their attack. If we don't watch for these lures, Satan will use them to take us off the track of God's leading. Like a deliberately misplaced detour sign, the enticements of pride and self-centeredness will mislead us into confusion and spiritual dysfunction—far from the path on which the Lord wants us to walk.

> ## "Why do you call Me, 'Lord, Lord,' and do not do what I say?"
>
> ### Luke 6:46

The life of king Saul (1 Samuel 15) quite graphically displays these characteristics. One of Saul's early tasks as king was to execute God's judgement on the Amalekites, the pagan tribe who ambushed defenseless Israel during the Exodus. Saul's assignment was to *"utterly destroy"* this heathen people, a severe but just punishment for their sinfulness. Deuteronomy calls such an assignment for merciless conquering as an instruction to put the enemy *"under a ban,"* and it involved killing every living being—man, woman, child, and beast—and destroying all their wealth and cities. Because the ungodly nation was so polluted by sin, nothing or no one was to be spared.

Saul and his men were not obedient to this directive, however. They killed the people (except for King Agag), and they destroyed everything that was worthless. But the good stuff—the sheep, oxen, etc.—they kept for themselves. They were only "partially obedient," which in God's eyes is still disobedience.

📖 Read 1 Samuel 15 and write what you learn in verse 11 about how Samuel followed through on what God had directed him to do.

> *I regret having made Saul king for he has turned from me and has not kept my command*

Notice what God says: *"He has turned back from following Me, and has not carried out My commands"* (1 Samuel 15:11). Notice God doesn't say, *"He only carried out part of My commands."* Partial obedience is still disobedience. If I obey God only when it doesn't conflict with my desires, I am not following God, but my own desires.

Why didn't Saul obey? To start with, why did he spare King Agag? Well, in that culture, the king of a conquered army was a trophy to be brought back and displayed. Often this conquered king was chained to the back of the conqueror's chariot to be paraded through town. The conquered king's humiliation intensified the victor's glory. Basically, humiliating Agag appealed to Saul's pride. He wanted to show off his success.

📖 Looking at verses 24 and 30, write what you see of Saul's pride and self-centeredness.

> *Saul replied to Samuel "I have sinned, for I have disobeyed the command of the Lord & your Instructions. In my fear of the people, I did what they said.*

We see his pride also in his explanation of why he didn't obey: *"Because I feared the people and listened to their voice"* (verse 24). He was more concerned with how he looked before the people than with pleasing God (verse 30). We see his self-centeredness in his rushing to take of the spoils rather than being totally obedient to God's command.

Did You Know?

UNDER THE BAN

The Hebrew word *charam* or *cherem* means "devoted" or "under the ban." Something put under the ban referred to something set aside totally for God's purposes. The spoils of Jericho were "devoted" or literally, "under the ban" – set apart, as it were, as firstfruits belonging to the Lord (Joshua 7). Leviticus 27:28 speaks of a devoted offering, and 27:29 speaks of a person under the ban, meaning that person was set apart for judgment to be executed for his sin. Amalek was among those under the ban ("utterly destroy"—1 Samuel 15:3, 8–9, 18, 20) whose crimes merited execution as did the Canaanites of Joshua's day.

The most telling aspect of this biblical vignette, however, is in how Saul responded once his sin was revealed. He displayed no remorse; he wasn't repentant about his sin. He wanted only to escape from the consequences (verses 25, 30). Saul was proud instead of humble (in fact, after his victory, he even set up a monument for himself—verse 12). Because he did not have a heart after God's heart (1 Samuel 13:13–14), he was rejected by God as king.

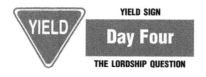

YIELD SIGN

Day Four

THE LORDSHIP QUESTION

PRIDE AND SELF-CENTEREDNESS

Pride often keeps us from yielding to God's will and way and hinders us from hearing Him. Along with its ugly stepsister, vanity, pride comes into play in our hearts by subtly whispering, "You are too good for that." Oh, it doesn't say it so plainly, but that is the message just the same. Pride constantly sets limitations on what God's will can be. Vanity usually causes us to be concerned about what others will think of us, or how something we do or say will look to others, or how a certain deed is beneath us. Both vanity and pride are stems from the same "sin tree."

The spirit and attitude of pride usually attaches conditions to God's will. When we are prideful, we offer God a list of the things we are unwilling to do and demand that He adjust His will accordingly. It's as if we hid a mental list in our hearts somewhere. Pride tells God, "I'll go into any vocation You lead me, but You can't lead me to one where I have to move some place I don't like"; or, "I'll do whatever you want me to do, as long as I don't have to stay single"; or some other conditional statement. Could Beth have been affected by this in her decision?

_____

_____

_____

_____

A sober lesson from King Saul's life is this:

Yieldedness with conditions attached to it is not yieldedness to God's will, but to ours. It is not deference to God's will and way, but to our own. From a Christian perspective, yieldedness is a state of yielding **everything** to God. If you are not surrendering **everything** to God, then you are not practicing true yieldedness.

📖 Look at James 4:6.

What does this verse teach us about God's attitude toward the proud?

"God resists the proud,
but gives grace to the humble"

_____

_____

_____

Yieldedness with conditions attached is not yieldedness.

What impact do you think this verse would have on that person hearing God?

Repent and humble yourself before God

God is opposed to the proud. He stands in constant opposition to such a person. Yet He is ever willing to give grace to the humble of heart. In James 1:5 we are told "... *if any of you lacks wisdom, let him ask of God, who gives to all men generously and without reproach.*" Yet in 1:8 James instructs us that we must ask rightly, for the double-minded man should not expect to receive anything from the Lord. Faith (trust) is one of the ways humility expresses itself, while double-mindedness (half for God and half for ourselves) is a reflection of a lack of surrender. If we want to hear God, we must settle that His way is what we really want.

Self-Centeredness

Closely related to pride and vanity is self-centeredness. Often we are simply too concerned with our own interest to take thought of what is important to God. Self-centeredness says, "I want to do. . ." and holds that as the supreme litmus for evaluating God's will. You'll never find God's will until you settle in your heart that you want to do it, whatever it is. If you want to know God's direction for a certain area of your life, then you better decide if you are willing to follow that direction, otherwise you are wasting your time—not to mention the Lord's time.

❖   ❖   ❖   ❖   ❖   ❖   ❖   ❖   ❖

Several weeks after her engagement, Beth called me and asked if we could get together. As we sat and shared Cokes™ at a diner, Beth flashed a large sparkling diamond at me and smilingly said, "Congratulate me!"

She told me of her engagement to Bob and asked if I would marry them. At first I was surprised, but Beth seemed intent enough that I had to take her seriously. "I'd love to hear how God led you to this decision," I replied, and immediately the mood shifted.

I hadn't meant it as a confrontation, but Beth's countenance told me I had touched a nerve. She became fidgety and nervous, and she related vague reasons for this being a good decision. Then she closed it off with, "I just have a real peace about it."

In retrospect, I am confident it was the Lord's prompting that led me to respond by asking rather abruptly, "What if Bob isn't the man God wants you to marry?" A mixture of shock and horror scurried across her face and she quickly retorted, "But I'm sure he is...he has to be!"

As I shared with Beth my interest in her welfare and my desire for her to experience God's best, I asked, "Honestly, how confident are you that this is God's will?"

"God is opposed to the proud, but gives grace to the humble"
—James 4:6

After an awkward moment's hesitation, she confided, "Oh, I guess about 75-percent sure."

She seemed relieved as I began to share with her some principles about God's will, and I encouraged her to continue asking God to confirm His leading. I asked, "Beth, would you mull over what I've shared and hold the decision until you can be 100-percent sure?" I also encouraged her to get away for the weekend where she could give her undistracted attention to the decision at hand and to the Lord.

A week later the Beth I met was a different person. Before a word passed her lips I could tell she had received her answer from the Lord. She began to relate to me her weekend with God; she had taken my advice and had asked God to line up the guideposts to His will. She shared with me the different counsel she had received and the time she spent "calculating the cost." She enthusiastically described her times in prayer and in the Scriptures, and how she applied the "sound mind" principle. "But the thing that turned the corner for me," she confessed, "was grappling with the **YIELD** sign."

Beth's eyes teared up as she began to share from her heart of coming to grips with the need to yield every area of her life to God's leading. "As I began talking honestly with God about various areas of my life, I realized that, though at one time my singleness had been yielded to God, in recent months I had taken it back from Him. I had begun to place marriage as a demand on God's will," she admitted.

As she realized this, she began to be honest with the Lord and tell Him of her desire to be married. She confessed, "Lord, in my heart, being married has become more important to me than following You."

Joy shone on her face as she shared how in this spirit of intercession she asked the Lord's forgiveness. She again affirmed to Him, "Lord, I want to be in Your will—even if that means I must remain single—because I know Your will is best. I know it will be good, acceptable, and perfect.

Once Beth yielded and gave her singleness back to the Lord, she began to see Bob in a different light. Although he offered her a steady relationship and financial security, Beth realized he probably would never share her love for Christ. She recognized that, unlike her, he would not want to seek the Lord's will in the major decisions life would bring. Instead of encouraging her in her walk with Christ, he would probably discourage it. "What I really want," she confided, "is a husband who will lead me spiritually. Now I'm willing to wait on the Lord and trust Him to give me the husband He wants me to have. For the first time in ages, I have peace in my heart." She was experiencing the delicious sense of God's rest, and she quietly mused that being married to a godly man was worth the wait.

> "... I realized that, though at one time my singleness had been yielded to God, in recent months I had taken it back from Him. I had begun to place marriage as a demand on God's will."
>
> —"Beth"

YIELD SIGN

Day Five

THE LORDSHIP QUESTION

FOR ME TO HEAR GOD

Where are you in your search for God's will? Can you identify with Beth and her circumstances? Are you confused about a certain situation and faced with making a decision? Consider the following questions as you evaluate where you are, and apply this first and most essential principle in determining God's will.

An Evaluation

1. Have I ever really surrendered my life to Jesus Christ as Lord and yielded myself to Him?

_____

_____

_____

_____

2. Am I willing to do God's will in this situation no matter what that is?

_____

_____

_____

3. Are my motives affected by pride? (Am I unwilling to do something "beneath" me?)

_____

_____

_____

_____

_____

_____

4. Are my motives affected by self-centered attitudes? (Am I placing my desires above God's?)

_____

_____

_____

_____

_____

_____

_____

 An Application

As you seek to discern God's will, you will find yourself at a fork in the road. One direction is God's way, the other is your own. They may not always look like different destinations—sometimes the destinations are the same—but the length of the trip and the means of getting there are different. You will never find God's will on the road to your own way.

So now you must decide, but you also must realize your decision will have consequences. If you decide to go your own way, God, as your loving heavenly Father, will discipline you, and He will continue to place **YIELD** signs in your path.

Surrender is the most important step in the process of hearing God. It demystifies the process of discerning His will.

On the other hand, if you choose His way, you must yield yourself to Him and trust that what He decides will be the best. But acknowledge this: you will never be disappointed, because God's will is filtered through His omniscience (He is all knowing); it is attended to by His omnipresence (He is ever present); and it is accomplished by His omnipotence (He is all powerful). Does your will have that much to offer?

Why not settle now that the Lord will be Lord in your life, and obey that **YIELD** sign? The following is a suggested prayer to affirm that decision. It isn't a magical prayer, and just saying the words won't change anything, but if you express this attitude in your heart to God, then you will be on the road to finding His will.

 A Prayer
Dear Lord, I want You to be the Lord of my life. I yield to You and trust that You know what is best. Whatever You want me to do in this decision, I am willing to do. The answer is yes; now You tell me the question. Help me to find Your will, and whatever it is, I'll do it. Amen.

Write your own prayer to the Lord in the space provided below.

_____

_____

_____

_____

_____

_____

_____

_____

_____

_____

Notes

Notes

THE TELEPHONE SIGNPOST:
A Study on Prayer

"Have you decided what you are going to do during the summer, Eddie?" my friend asked. I was a freshman in college and Mack had led me to Christ a few months earlier. Since then I had leaned on his advice in spiritual matters, and in an informal way he was discipling me. He watched out for my spiritual welfare with the tender concern God gives a servant when He uses him to birth a new believer.

"What do you think about going on the beach project?" he asked with genuine interest.

A few days earlier he had told me about a summer mission project with the campus ministry in which we were involved. One of these projects had been very significant in his spiritual growth, and he had challenged me to consider if this was something God would want me to do.

"I don't think I'm going to do that," I replied. "I'm leaning toward working at that Christian camp with Eric" (a mutual friend).

"Have you prayed about it?" he questioned.

"No, to be honest, I haven't."

"Have you prayed about it?"

I guess it hadn't really dawned on me that I could ask God what He wanted me to do. As a new Christian, I knew God had a moral will for me, and I was trying to learn what pleased Him. However, I didn't yet understand that He could lead me even in the smaller decisions of my life. Yet, the idea of God leading me made some sense to me. After all, hadn't I read in the Bible to *"pray without ceasing"* (1 Thess. 5:17).

"I'll take some time to pray about it before I decide," I assured him.

As I lay in bed that night, I remembered my commitment and began bringing the matter before the Lord. "God," I prayed, "I'm not sure what to do." I had pretty much decided to take a job as a counselor at the camp. It was situated in the Smoky Mountains near my home, and I loved the outdoors; so I was excited about the prospect of spending my summer hiking, camping, and canoeing—and getting paid for it! The fact that it was a Christian camp was the icing on the cake. Surely God would be pleased if I did something Christian with my summer. It made perfect sense to me. Trouble is, I hadn't asked God what He wanted me to do. As I realized that, I entreated, "What should I do, Lord?"

TELEPHONE SIGN

Day One

PRAYER

THE NEED FOR PRAYER

O ne near-fatal flaw we human beings have is our innate tendency to "lean on our own understanding." I'm not saying a Christian unplugs his brain when he seeks God's will, but the admonition of Proverbs 3:5–6 makes it clear that limited, finite, human reasoning isn't adequate for all the decisions we are called to make.

📖 Read Proverbs 3:5–6 and answer the questions that follow.

What is being contrasted with trusting the Lord in these verses?

Trusting the Lord or doing things "our" way

What do you think it means to "lean" on your own understanding?

To follow the word and not consult God

How do we *"acknowledge Him"* in all our ways?

By lifting things up to Him and communicating with Him

Word Study
PROVERBS 3:5–6

Sha'an ("lean")—to lean against, to cause to support oneself. This verb depicts an attitude of trust.

Yadha ("acknowledge")—to perceive, to understand, to acquire knowledge, to be familiar with, to be aware of.

'Orach ("paths")—this noun is normally translated "way" or "path." Most often it is used figuratively.

Yashar ("straight")—to be level, to make straight, to declare right. This word has two main meanings: literally (straight), and ethically (upright and moral).

What is the result?

He guides us and gives us peace

Here in Proverbs 3 we see trusting the Lord contrasted with leaning on or trusting our own understanding. The Hebrew word for *lean* means "to support oneself." It doesn't mean that we don't use our own understanding; rather, it says that human logic alone is not sufficient to support us. The admonition to acknowledge Him in all our ways makes it clear that in every situation life brings our way, there is a need to bring that situation to the Lord through prayer. We must lean on the Lord and ask His wisdom in all our decisions. Then He will direct our paths.

The second signpost we encounter on this road to God's will is the **TELE-PHONE** sign. It is divinely designed to remind us of our need to "call home"—to ask our heavenly Father what to do and where to go.

📖 Look at Jeremiah 33:3.

What is the invitation of this verse?
Call to the Lord

What is the promise?
He will tell us great things that we do not know

In Jeremiah 33:3 we read: *"Call to me, and I will answer you, and I will tell you great and mighty things, which you do not know."* Some identify this reference as "God's phone number" because of its open invitation to "call to God." The promise here is that if we will call upon Him, He will answer us and tell us things we do not already know.

📖 In James 1:5 we find an incredible promise. Look at the verse and answer the questions that follow.

Who is invited to ask of God?
Those who lack wisdom

To whom will God give answers?
Those who ask in faith, not doubting

> **God's Telephone Number: Jeremiah 33:3—"Call to me, and I will answer you, and I will tell you great and mighty things, which you do not know."**

How does God give answers?

_____

_____

_____

> "I find that the chief purpose of prayer in determining the will of God is to get my will in an unprejudiced state about the issue at hand."
>
> —John Wesley

God wants us to know His will, but He isn't going to force it on us. We must, in faith, ask Him for it, and when we do, He fulfills His promise. Anyone who lacks wisdom is invited to ask God, and the promise is that He will give it to all. God's giving of wisdom when He is asked is not done begrudgingly or sparingly, but generously and without reproach.

One might well say that prayer is the ignition key to fire up the process of finding God's will. We cannot expect God to give us the wisdom we lack if we haven't even asked Him for it. Once we do ask, we can begin looking for His answer. But how does He reveal His answer? That is what the rest of this book details. Each of the remaining signposts shows us where to look for God's answers to the prayer in James 1:5. John Wesley put it this way:

> I find that the chief purpose of prayer in determining the will of God is to get my will in an unprejudiced state about the issue at hand. Then, when my will is unprejudiced, I find that God suggests reasons to my mind concerning the proper course.

TELEPHONE SIGN

Day Two

PRAYER

THE OPPORTUNITY OF PRAYER

It is amazing how easily we forget to pray. Like I did with my summer decision as a new Christian, we often forget what a resource God is for our decisions. In Hebrews 10:19–22 we see the Old Testament high priest coming into the presence of God contrasted with how the believer accesses God's presence today. The high priest could only go into the Holy of Holies once a year in fear and trembling. He came through the blood of a bull which could not take away sin, but only cover it. How different it is for us today!

📖 Read Hebrews 10:19–22.

How is our entering of the Holy Place in the New Testament different than the experience of the priest?

Jesus Christ took all our sins by dying on the cross for us.

What is it that allows us into God's presence?

Christ having died for our sins.

What should our response be to this privilege (v. 22)?

Approach God with a sincere heart and in absolute trust

God's presence is always open to us. Though in Old Testament times the priest entered the Holy of Holies (God's presence) once a year in fear and trembling (*Yom Kippur*), today we can enter into God's presence at any time, with confidence, through the blood of Christ (Hebrews 10:19). Yet most believers rarely exercise this incredible privilege. *"Let us draw near. . ."* the writer tells us.

But what if we draw near in a wrong way? What if our attitude is wrong? Will God still hear our prayers then? I think if each of us is honest we would have to admit that sometimes we don't come to the Lord in prayer because we do not feel worthy, or we do not think He hears because we know our attitude is not right.

📖 Look at Psalm 55:17 and write what you learn about the types of prayers God will hear.

All prayers

What an amazing verse! It is incredible to think that because God is my heavenly Father, He hears all that I say. Even when my prayers are filled with complaining and murmuring He still hears them. When we understand the reality of Hebrews 10—that we have access to the presence of God with confidence through the blood of Jesus—then we can begin to comprehend that it is not our worthiness that causes God to hear our prayers. <u>It is the worthiness of Christ, not our worthiness, that causes God to hear.</u> That is why we pray in Jesus' name instead of in our own name.

📖 Look at the verses below in light of what you have seen, and write what you learn about how God views your prayers.

Proverbs 15:8

He delights in the prayer of the upright.

Proverbs 15:29

The prayer of the just he hears

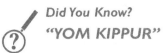

Did You Know?
"YOM KIPPUR"

The High Priest was allowed past the veil of the temple only once a year on *Yom Kippur*, the Day of Atonement. He would enter into the Holy of Holies to sprinkle sacrificial blood on the mercy seat to atone for the sins of the nation. While he was inside, the nation would wait in silence. When he went inside, a rope would be tied to his ankle, for if his sacrifice was not acceptable, he would die in the presence of the Lord, and no one could go inside to retrieve the body. The hem of his robe was strung with bells, and the attendants could hear him moving around. This was their reassurance that he was still alive. When he came outside, the nation would cheer, for this was the proof that their sins were atoned.

> ## "The prayer of the upright is His delight."
> ### Proverbs 15:8

In Proverbs 15:8 we see that the *"prayer of the upright is His delight."* In other words, God takes delight in hearing what we have to say to Him. As a proud father at the simple words of a toddler, it is not the flowery words or proper language that make God turn His ear to us, but His parental love. Proverbs 15:29 echos this idea, affirming that He hears the prayers of the righteous—in other words, the prayers of those with a right relationship to Him.

If we want to know God's will, we must ask Him for it. We will not discern it through simple human reasoning. As someone once said, "There is a lot you can do once you have prayed, but you can do nothing until you pray." If we run about trying to solve problems without first listening to God, we will be following ourselves like a dog chasing its own tail, and we will get nowhere. But clearly, God has granted us the opportunity to pray.

TELEPHONE SIGN

Day Three

PRAYER

THE PRACTICE OF PRAYER

It may seem a bit elementary to discuss the actual practice of prayer. I realize you may have cut your spiritual teeth on "Now I lay me down to sleep. . . ." Prayer is simple, isn't it? Or is it? What I have observed in my ministry through the years is that most people perceive prayer as a ritual: kneeling and/or bowing the head, folding the hands, reciting a grocery list of requests interspersed with sixteenth-century English perhaps out of reverence for God or perhaps because we believe that is how God talks. Yet most of us really don't understand prayer as a fundamental part of a relationship with God.

Certain aspects of our faith are fundamental, things we never outgrow. We apply these things every day regardless of how mature we are in Christ. Prayer is one such fundamental. I am reminded of the great football coach, Vince Lombardi, who started the first practice of every season with the same line: "This is a football." His message was loud and clear—success isn't found in the flashy stuff, but in the fundamentals. The same is true in our spiritual lives.

The Fundamentals of Prayer

The first fundamental of prayer is that it is simply communicating with God from our hearts. Because of this, there is no such thing as an insincere prayer. If it isn't from our hearts, it isn't prayer, even if we call it that. It is only "lip-service." Like me, you have probably sat through prayer meetings where you wondered if any of the words even made it past the ceiling.

Unfortunately, many prayers offered in our prayer meetings are merely sermonettes to each other. Sadly, we worry so much about wording our prayer the right way (to impress others) that we forget we are talking to God. We fail to realize He isn't concerned about the wording as much as He is about our attitude. So the first fundamental of prayer is that **it must be honest communication from our hearts to the heart of God.**

📖 Read Matthew 6:5.

What does Jesus call the person who prays to be heard by those around him?

Hypocrites

What is the outcome of such praying?

> *Others notice the praying and that is their reward.*

The one who prays with a view to being heard by those around him, Jesus calls a hypocrite. Jesus makes it clear that when we pray to be noticed by others, the only reward we will have is that we are noticed by others. We are not noticed by God.

The second fundamental of prayer is that, contrary to the teachings of many, **there is no power in the prayer itself.** Before you start tying me to the stake and piling up the brush, let me explain. Often we profess and promote the erroneous idea that prayer has some intrinsic power in itself. We wrongly place our faith in prayer instead of in God. This false doctrine's roots derive more from Eastern mysticism and the New Age movement than from biblical Christianity. True prayer is powerful only because God is powerful. The real power of prayer is our connection with the all-powerful Creator. Prayer is not a means of twisting God's arm, but of communicating with Him openly.

📖 Read Matthew 6:7.

What do the Gentiles (unbelievers in this case) trust to be heard by God?

> *They babble and think they will be heard cause of their many words.*

Pagans wrongly think that there is some mystical power in spoken words. They think if the prayer is long enough or wordy enough, somehow that will make it more acceptable to any deities that might happen to be listening. But clearly they are wrong. Jesus says, *"do not use meaningless repetition as the Gentiles do."* There is no power in the act of praying, only in the One we pray to.

The third fundamental of prayer is that **nothing is off-limits.** We can (and should) pray about anything and everything. A great passage to educate us on the proper practice of prayer is Philippians 4:6: *"Be anxious for nothing, but in everything by prayer and supplication with thanksgiving let your requests be made known to God."* Here we find specific directions on how to proceed in prayer.

📖 Look at each phrase in Philippians 4:6–7 and write your thoughts in the space provided.

"Be anxious for nothing. . . ."

> *We should be in dialog with God at all times about everything*

True prayer is powerful only because God is powerful.

". . . but in everything. . . ."

Nothing is too small or insignificant for God

". . . by prayer and supplication. . . ."

We can be specific about our requests to God

". . . with thanksgiving. . . ."

Always give God the gratitude he is owed.

". . . let your requests be made known to God."

First, we must **choose to lay aside our anxiety.** Anxiety should always be viewed as a red flag alerting us to the need to pray. Anxiety or worry can be a direct result of my trusting in myself and my own resources instead of in God. There are no guarantees that I will never be anxious, but if I let it dictate my response to God, it is sin, and it should be dealt with as such. Next, the boundaries of prayer are given: **in everything.** No matter how much we weasel and squirm, we cannot escape the reality that God wants us to talk with Him about everything, every area of our lives. Anything less is disobedience. The third step in our process of prayer is **to pray.** This may sound silly, but the passage gives us specifics on how to go about this. First Paul says, *"in everything by* **prayer."** These words relate to the means of general prayer directed to God. Next he says, *"and* **supplication."** The term supplication implies praying for particular benefits, in other words, making our requests specific. Next, we are told to accompany these requests with **thanksgiving.** When we lay aside anxiety and pray for everything (including specific requests) in an attitude of thanksgiving, we can make any request of God we desire—for any thing! Sound too good to be true? No, it is simply God's invitation to honesty. He wants us to bare our hearts to Him.

We must notice, however, that there is no promise God will give us our request. Sound unfair? Actually, what God promises is even better. Instead of promising to honor our request, regardless of whether it is beneficial to us or not, God promises to guard our hearts with His peace (Philippians 4:7). How does He do that? When we follow the specific formula of Philippians 4:6–7, we are, in essence, laying our request at God's feet. Once we've done that, we can have confidence that He hears us (Psalm 4:3). We can know that

Ask yourself, "Do I really want what my all-loving, all-knowing heavenly Father says is not the best for me?"

if our request is within His will, He'll give it to us. If not, He'll say no. Either way we can have peace because our request has now been filtered through God's will for us, which is *"good . . . acceptable and perfect"* (Romans 12:2).

But what if God's will is not what I want? Ask yourself this: "Do I really want what my all-loving, all-knowing heavenly Father says is not the best for me?" Are you willing to settle for something less than God's will?

BARRIERS TO OBEYING THIS SIGN

📖 Big barriers to obeying the call to prayer are found in James 4:2. Read this verse and write what you learn about barriers to obeying this signpost to hearing God.

_____

_____

_____

_____

_____

The first barrier James mentions is that we do not have . . . because we do not ask. This was my problem in the summer missions decision I mentioned at the beginning of this lesson. Often, we simply try to figure out our own solutions instead of asking God for His. We strive to get what we want in our own way instead of looking to God. You may be saying, "But I have asked, and I still don't have." Let's analyze. In light of our fundamentals of true prayer, did your request really connect your faith to God, or did you place your faith in prayer? The difference is subtle but significant.

📖 Now look at James 4:3 and identify the barrier it gives.

<u>Wrong motives</u>_____

_____

_____

A second barrier James mentions is that we do ask, but we ask with wrong motives. We don't really want God's will, we only want our own pleasure. This may be physical or emotional pleasure—the pleasure of a trial-free, work-free existence. In any case, this wrong motive violates the necessary call to lordship we discussed in Lesson One. It is a commitment to our will instead of God's.

As I thought about the beach project my friend Mack had challenged me to, I ran into a lot of obstacles. *I am a really young Christian,* I thought. *What if I apply and don't get accepted?*

"You do not have because you do not ask. You ask and do not receive, because you ask with wrong motives, so that you may spend it on your pleasures."

James 4:2–3

"but let him ask in faith...."

James 1:6

Most pressing, though, was the fact that in order to apply, I would have to pay a $15 nonrefundable registration fee. For a guy working his way through college in the 1970s, that was a lot of money—more money than I had to spare! I prayed, "Lord, if You want me to go on this summer missions project, You'll have to provide the fifteen dollars." That seemed an easy way to find the answer.

The next day was payday on my part-time job. I already had calculated the hours I had worked, and the check would be just barely enough to cover my bills and see me through to the next payday. Imagine my surprise when the check I picked up was fifteen dollars more than what I had expected. Turns out, my employer had made a mistake on a previous check and was making it up. "There's the fifteen dollars I prayed for!" I shouted to my roommate, as surprised that God answered my prayer as I was with how He did it.

I sent my application in and waited. I still wasn't fully convinced though. I thought, *After all this, what if I really don't get accepted?* So I did not turn down the camp job. On the summer project application they said they would let me know by April 10, and the camp director extended the final deadline for a decision until then. But April 10 came and I still hadn't heard from the summer project. "What should I do, Lord?" I prayed once again, frantically seeking an answer.

At that point, the Holy Spirit brought to mind what I had prayed the first time: "Lord, if You want me to go on this summer missions project, You'll have to provide the fifteen dollars." God had already given me my answer. I just had to take Him at His word and trust Him. Remember, James 1:6 says I must ask in faith. Even though I had no acceptance in hand, I did have God's leading, so I turned down the camp job. A few days later my summer project acceptance arrived, and that summer changed my life. It was the most intense time of spiritual growth I had experienced. It was one of many ways the Lord has showed me and reminded me that His will is *"good . . . acceptable and perfect"* (Romans 12:2).

TELEPHONE SIGN

Day Five

PRAYER

PUTTING IT INTO PRACTICE

One of the surest ways to guarantee a small crowd at church is to call a prayer meeting. People will stay away in droves. Why is that? Why do we find it easier to do everything else in the Christian life besides prayer? First, I believe one of the things that keeps us from prayer is the fact that it is work. It requires focus to talk to God instead of talking to ourselves or those around us. Second, I think prayer is difficult because we expect it to be. We have been conditioned to dread prayer because of religious activities that were mere ritual. I am amazed at how people seem to enjoy a message that makes them feel bad about their prayer life. It is not so much that they expect anything to change, as it is that they assume everyone else has a better prayer life than they have, yet they possess no hope that their prayer life will ever change for he better. The next best thing, in their minds, to a good prayer life is at least feeling bad about not having one. But prayer shouldn't be that way. It is an opportunity and a priviledge, not a burden. We just need to be able to separate it from the religious rituals that mascarade for true prayer.

APPLY As you seek to apply this important area to hearing God, it is important to first evaluate where you are. Look at the list below and check the areas where you feel you are struggling.

___ I'm so used to doing things myself that I don't remember to talk to God about it.

___ I don't really see the need to pray.

___ I'm not sure that God really listens.

___ I don't feel worthy.

___ It hasn't seemed to work in the past.

___ I forget.

___ I lean too much on my own understanding (see Prov. 3:5).

___ I tend to pray selfishly instead of in surrendered fashion.

_✓_ Instead of laying aside all anxieties, I worry.

Take a look the areas above where you are struggling. What do you think you need to do about those areas in light of what we have studied this week?

I completely trust in God but my anxiety and worry seems to always creep in. I have to be more deliberate and disciplined to lay them aside and pray whole heartedly.

When circumstances arise, how often do you pray about them before doing anything else?

Never_____

Rarely_____

Sometimes_____

Often_____

Always_ ✓ _

We identified some specific steps to follow in praying for God's will as found in Philippians 4:6–7:

☑ I must choose to lay aside my anxiety.

☑ I must transfer my trust from myself to God.

☑ I must openly discuss every area with God.

☑ I must direct my prayer to Him in a specific manner and accompany it with thanksgiving.

☑ I may then bring **any** request to Him.

☑ I must trust Him for His peace and accept His answer, whatever it is.

Take a few minutes now to express your prayer for wisdom in writing to the Lord in the spaces provided below:

Lay aside anxiety. . .

My biggest stumbling block.

Openly discuss every area in a specific manner...

Accompany it with thanksgiving...

I try to do this always

Bring your <u>request</u> (what <u>you</u> desire)...

Sometimes I tell Him what I think my answer should look like.

Trust Him for peace to guard your heart...

Accept His answer.

Amen.

This is how we use prayer to turn our ear toward heaven.

Notes

Notes

THE "TURN ON YOUR HEADLIGHTS" SIGN:
The Illumination of Scripture

"I just wish I knew what to do," Steve exclaimed with sincerity. Although he had been a believer for almost a year, he had been dating Susan since high school, and they were planning to get married as soon as they both finished college. It had never occurred to Steve that God might not approve of their relationship. Never, that is, until his pastor confronted him the week before. "Steve, you have to break up with her," he said. "She's not a Christian, and God would never bless that kind of marriage."

He went away crushed. "I mean, it's not like we've been sleeping together or anything," he exclaimed. "Neither of us wants that until marriage. My dad says I should ignore him. He says the preacher is just legalistic. What do you think, Eddie?" he inquired.

Although I wasn't discipling Steve, we had often talked of our common faith in Christ, and it wasn't unusual for him to ask me questions about the Bible. This was different though. This wasn't some idle curiosity about Old Testament history or wondering where a certain verse was located. Steve was desperate for understanding and counsel, and he needed more of an answer than his pastor was giving him. He liked his church because of the friends

> *"All Scripture is inspired by God and profitable for teaching, for reproof, for correction, for training in righteousness; that the man of God may be adequate, equipped for every good work."*
>
> **2 Timothy 3:16–17**

he had made there, but often he questioned what the pastor taught, so I wasn't surprised Steve didn't jump at his advice. "Do you think God will refuse to bless our marriage just because Susan isn't a Christian?" Steve asked earnestly.

What would you say to Steve? Would you agree with the pastor and tell him God wouldn't bless his marriage to a non-Christian? Or would you tell him that as long as their relationship was morally okay, they could pursue it as far as they wanted? Or would you sweep the whole issue under the rug and say, "God will show you in time"? What would you say?

Steve needed more than simple opinions. He needed real answers, authoritative answers. Fortunately, God's will is not merely an issue of picking the opinion that sounds the best. God has given us His Word, which moves us from subjective opinions to objective authority. That is what this signpost is all about.

HEADLIGHTS SIGN
Day One
ILLUMINATION OF SCRIPTURE

TURN ON HEADLIGHTS

WALKING IN THE LIGHT

As we continue on our road to God's will, we encounter a sign which reads **TURN ON YOUR HEADLIGHTS**. I remember as a child seeing such a sign at the entrance to one of my favorite road trip attractions: the tunnel. Back in the days before Disney World and Darth Vader, that was big-time entertainment. And if we were really lucky, we'd experience the ultimate of thrills—Dad would honk the horn! I realize that isn't nearly so big a deal for my kids and possibly not for you either, but perhaps like me, you have encountered a **TURN ON YOUR HEADLIGHTS** sign and found yourself wondering why people need to be reminded to do this. Truth is, dangerous as it is to drive in the dark without your headlights on, people still do it sometimes.

📖 This principle applies to our spiritual lives as well. Read Psalm 119:105 and answer the questions that follow.

Think about what this verse is saying. In your own words, write out the picture the author is trying to paint as an analogy of how the Word works.

_____
_____
_____
_____
_____
_____

In what ways does the Word of God function as a "lamp to our feet" on a darkened path?

_____
_____
_____

"Thy word is a lamp to my feet, And a light to my path."
—Psalm 119:105

God's Word is intended to illumine our way, yet so often in the midst of our need we forget to "turn on our headlights." Instead of going to God's Word for direction, we look elsewhere. *"God is light"* (1 John 1:5), and anything else, no matter how bright it appears, is darkness. What Steve needed was not the confusion of sorting through conflicting opinions, but the light and direction of God's Word.

The description of the working of God's Word we find in Psalm 119:105 pictures the spiritual truth of the illuminating work of Scripture. Consider the analogy. You are walking along a path at night with a lamp to show your way. The lamp doesn't illumine the path in its entirety. It merely creates a circle of light large enough to show you the next few steps on the path. It gives enough light to keep you from stumbling, but not so much that you are distracted from watching your step.

The Workings of God's Will

Not only does this analogy illustrate the working of God's Word, but it also gives clarity to understanding God's will. He doesn't reveal it in one big lump, but a little bit at a time. Paul Little, in his booklet *Affirming the Will of God* (InterVaristy Press, 1999), expresses it this way:

> The will of God is not like a magic package let down from heaven by a string. . . . the will of God is far more like a scroll that unrolls every day. . . . the will of God is something to be discerned and lived out every day of our lives. It is not something to be grasped as a package once for all. Our call, therefore, is basically not to follow a plan or a blueprint, or to go to a place or take up a work, but rather to follow the Lord Jesus Christ.

One of the key ways we "follow the Lord Jesus Christ" is by living according to His Word.

📖 Look up the verses listed below and write what they teach about the light-giving properties of the Word of God.

Psalm 19:8

_____

_____

_____

_____

Psalm 43:3

_____

_____

_____

_____

Psalm 119:130

_____

_____

_____

_____

> *"Our call, . . . is basically not to follow a plan or a blueprint, or to go to a place or take up a work, but rather to follow the Lord Jesus Christ."*
>
> **—Paul Little**
> **Affirming the Will of God**
> **InterVarsity Press, 1999**

_____

_____

_____

_____

_____

Psalm 19:8 makes a simple, yet profound statement: *"The commandment of the Lord is pure, enlightening the eyes."* In other words, because it is pure, it can give light. Psalm 43:3 picks up this idea, as it equates light and truth. It is a prayer for the Lord to use that light to lead. As Psalm 119:130 puts it: *"The unfolding of Thy words gives light; It gives understanding to the simple."* If you are like me, nothing makes you feel "simple" like trying to discern God's will. But, as Steve was about to find out, God's Word has the solution to that need. The last passage is perhaps the most profound. Jesus makes it clear in John 3:19–21 that we will not come to the light God gives if our heart is bent toward doing evil. In fact, it is our choices to practice truth that keep moving us toward the light.

HEADLIGHTS SIGN

Day Two

ILLUMINATION OF SCRIPTURE

FOLLOWING GOD THROUGH HIS WORD

So how exactly do we follow God through His Word? To begin with, we must acknowledge one essential reality. Although you are probably grasping these principles of determining God's will in one specific area, it is imperative you realize that you will spend the rest of your Christian life seeking and finding the will of God. If our call is to follow Christ, then we will never outgrow our need to know His will. Because of this, let me suggest that the application really needs to be on two different levels.

First, like Steve, you probably have a present need to know God's will, and to meet it you will need to find Scriptures that address it. Some of these will be clear commands as to what the believer can and cannot do. Many of them, however, will give you principles that are to guide and direct you.

Because of this present need, you may want some help in finding these Scriptures. Two Bible tools will be helpful. An exhaustive concordance will help you find that verse you sort of remember but aren't sure where it is. The other resource is a topical Bible (such as *Nave's*). You can now find plenty of resources such as these with computer software "Bible-on-CD" programs and via the Internet. Perhaps you can borrow a book format copy from your pastor or a friend, or pick one up at your local Christian bookstore. Bible tools such as these will help you find passages involving the key topics you are considering. For example, if you are seeking God's will about marriage, it would be important to see what God's Word says about this subject.

Another resource in finding relevant passages will come from the counsel of godly Christians. We will take a thorough look at this resource in the next chapter.

As we seek to follow God through His Word, we will find answers to our immediate need, but since we will always be needing to find God's will, our present study of the Scriptures also lays a foundation for future insight.

📖 Read Psalm 37:31 and write what you learn there about the results of being in God's Word.

_____

_____

_____

_____

_____

David relates this in Psalm 37:31: *"The law of his God is in his heart; His steps do not slip."* The Word not only offers prescriptive answers for our present need, but works as preventive medicine for our future needs as well. This is what Paul had in mind in Romans 12:1 and 2 when he spoke of the transforming work of a "renewed" mind. He was referring to a mind that is deepening in the Word of God.

But what about areas where there is no "Thou shalt" or "Thou shalt not"? How do we determine God's will in the areas Scripture doesn't address? To begin with, let me emphasize that Scripture addresses life much more broadly than most people realize. Perhaps my counsel to Steve will help illustrate some the many different ways God's Word speaks to our need.

"Steve, first of all, I don't want to just pile my opinion on top of everyone else's. I believe the Bible has a lot to say about this, and I think, instead of listening to me or anyone else, you ought to let the Scriptures tell you what to do." To start with, I directed him to Acts 17:11–12. "Here is a good attitude to have about Christian advice," I said as I showed him the Berean Christians' example:

> *Now these* [the Bereans] *were more noble-minded than those in Thessalonica, for they received the word with great eagerness, examining the Scriptures daily, to see whether these things were so. Many of them therefore believed.*

📖 Look at this verse and see if you can find the three things that set the Bereans apart.

_____

_____

_____

_____

Three important things set the Bereans apart. First, they were eager for the truth. They didn't just want their ears tickled and their preconceptions supported. Second, they checked out everything for themselves in the Bible. Too many Christians only know what their pastor tells them of the Bible. They never check it out for themselves. Finally, they were willing to act on what they learned. "Many of them therefore believed."

> **"Now these were more noble-minded than those in Thessalonica, for they received the word with great eagerness, examining the Scriptures daily, to see whether these things were so."**
>
> **Acts 17:11**

> *"Many of them therefore believed, along with a number of prominent Greek women and men."*
>
> *Acts 17:12*

📖 Read the verses listed below and write what you learn from them about how the Scriptures relate to knowing God's will.

Romans 12:1–2

_____

_____

_____

_____

_____

_____

Psalm 40:8

_____

_____

_____

_____

_____

Romans 12:1–2 is a very familiar passage to many of us, but we must guard against allowing familiarity to dim the significance of what is said there. Not only does surrender play an important part in us being able to "prove what the will of God is," but also in cultivating within us a renewed mind. Scripture gives a new perspective—a new way of thinking. In Psalm 40:8 we pick up an important additional thought: Not only does Scripture help us to determine God's will, it also helps us to desire it.

TURN ON HEADLIGHTS

HEADLIGHTS SIGN

Day Three

ILLUMINATION OF SCRIPTURE

How the Bible Speaks to Us

As I was trying to help my friend Steve, I found one thing that really helped his view of the Word was understanding how the Scriptures speak. Sadly, many of us only think of the Bible as a book of "do's and don'ts." While the Scriptures do set some boundaries for the Lord in how we are to live, it has far more to offer than just that.

"Now, Steve," I said, "the Bible can speak to us in four different ways, and I believe it uses all of them on this important issue of whom to marry. Sometimes the Bible gives us clear commands, **proclamations** such as, 'Thou shalt' <u>do</u> something. Another way the Bible speaks to us is through **prohibitions.** This is when the Scripture says, 'Thou shalt <u>not</u>' in a clear way. The third way Scripture speaks is through **promises.** Fourth, God's Word speaks to our need in the form of **principles,** wisdom from understanding how life is 'wired.' Let me share some passages with you that speak in these ways."

I want to share with you what I shared with Steve, but I also want you to get involved with the process, so I am going to weave some Bible study examples into it so you can see these truths for yourself. When we look at this area of whom to marry, I want you to see the four different ways the Bible addresses that one question.

Principles

📖 Look at Numbers 25:1–9 and answer the questions that follow.

What was the sin that Israel committed?

_____

_____

What was the consequence?

_____

_____

_____

📖 Now look at Numbers 31:15–16. What was behind the intermarriage with the daughters of Moab, which resulted in God's judgment?

_____

_____

_____

_____

In Numbers 25 we can draw out some excellent principles on why it might not be wise to marry an unbeliever. It is the story of Balaam, a prophet of God who was hired to curse Israel. God wouldn't let him bring a curse on Israel, but because Balaam still wanted the pagan king's money, he apparently clued him in to how he could undermine Israel and lessen their threat: "Simply have your daughters intermarry with their sons and soon they will be no threat to you."

As Numbers 25 relates, it worked. Soon, instead of following God, Israel's sons followed their pagan wives into idol worship. In almost every biblical instance of believers marrying unbelievers, it is not the unbelieving spouse who is pulled up, but the believing spouse who is pulled down. (See Deuteronomy 7:1–4.)

Many other principles recorded in Scripture address this issue as well. Principles don't come out and say "Steve, thou shalt not marry so-and-so," but they do give us wisdom through observing the principle behind the story.

Promises

📖 Another way Scripture speaks to this question of who to marry is through promises. Look at the verses below from Proverbs 31 and identify the promises you find there.

31:10

_____

_____

_____

_____

Doctrine

HOW THE BIBLE SPEAKS

proclamations—clear commands

prohibitions—the "Thou shalt nots"

promises—"if, then" passages

principles—wisdom from life

31:11

_____

_____

_____

_____

31:12

_____

_____

_____

_____

In Proverbs 31 we see some of the many blessings for a man who is married to *"a woman who fears the Lord."* We see that her worth is *"far above jewels"* (verse 10). Her husband will have no lack of gain (verse 11). This type of wife will do her husband good and not evil all her life (verse 12). This positively affirms why it is worth it to wait for God to provide a believing wife. It relates the many joys you will be robbed of if you don't marry a believer. If we want the blessing of the promises we must obey the direction they point us toward.

Prohibitions

A third way Scripture speaks to this question of who to marry is through prohibitions. Read 2 Corinthians 6:14–18.

What is the specific prohibition here?

_____

_____

_____

_____

What are the reasons given for it?

_____

_____

_____

_____

Perhaps the most familiar passage related on this subject of marriage is found in 2 Corinthians 6:14–18. Here the believer is very clearly admonished not to be unequally yoked with an unbeliever. A formal (legal) bond with an unbeliever, be it through marriage, business partnership, or whatever, is unacceptable for the Christian. The analogy here of being unequally yoked offers a graphic agricultural picture of the problems of such a relationship. Two undesirable results are described when a team of oxen are unequally yoked (a strong ox with a smaller, weaker one): Either the imbalance will cause the team to plow crooked, or the stronger ox will have to go slow since the weaker one is unable to keep pace.

If we want the blessing of the promises we must obey the directions toward which the promises point.

Proclamations

Read 1 Corinthians 7:39 and identify the proclamation there concerning marriage.

_____

_____

_____

_____

_____

_____

Finally, Scripture speaks to this question of whom to marry through proclamations or positive commands. In 1 Corinthians 7:39 we learn that a widow, once her husband is dead, is free to marry whomever she wishes—with one restriction: *"only in the Lord."* She may remarry, but only a believer.

So, where did this leave Steve? Although the Bible doesn't address every issue this thoroughly, the Scriptures had clearly shown from all angles that a believer marrying an unbeliever is not God's will. So he had his answer, right? Well maybe, and maybe not. You see, his question wasn't, "Can a Christian marry a non-Christian?" Rather, it was, "Is it okay for me to marry Susan?" As we conversed, I shared with him that very clearly he could not marry Susan, an unbeliever, and be following God's will, but that didn't mean Susan wouldn't come to share his faith in Christ. Steve didn't need an oversimplified answer and I wasn't going to give him one.

"Steve, here is my advice," I related. "First, realize that perhaps God has placed you in Susan's life so that she might hear and see the truth of God's love. Of all people, you should be the first to share with her the good news of Jesus Christ. If I were you, I would take some time to explain to her how you came to know the Lord and what He means to you.

"Second, if she still isn't interested in spiritual things, something that is so important to you, then you have some hard choices to make. You're already 'unequally yoked' by dating her, and to continue in that relationship as it is will hinder your walk with Christ, not help it.

"Finally," I continued, "you need to be careful that you don't push Susan into an insincere commitment only to justify your marrying her. You need to make sure there is evidence of her being a new creature in Christ before you go any further in this relationship. Remember, Steve, God's will for you is 'good, acceptable, and perfect' (see Romans 12:2). If He doesn't want you to marry Susan, then His will for you will definitely be better. Don't shortchange yourself by settling for anything less than God's best."

As you can see from the above discussion, the Word of God speaks much more broadly to life than we sometimes think. Even if the Bible has no "Thou shalts" or "Thou shalt nots" to speak to our circumstances, there are principles that always relate.

God has not left us to make life's decisions in the dark. We have the light of His Word to illumine our feet and light our path.

> *Even if the Bible has no "Thou shalts" or "Thou shalt nots" to speak to our circumstances, there are principles that always relate.*

BARRIERS TO OBEYING THIS SIGN

As we look at the signposts of Scripture, it will help us if we consider some of the roadblocks that hinder our obedience to these principles. The clear leading of God by itself doesn't guarantee the believer will always be on the right track. We must accurately interpret God's leading, and we must choose to follow it. There are several potential barriers to our obeying this sign.

📖 Look at 2 Timothy 2:15. What is the implied warning in this verse?

_____

_____

_____

The most significant barrier to our obedience is the danger of **mishandling God's Word.** Paul exhorted his disciple, the young pastor Timothy, *"Be diligent to present yourself approved to God as a workman who does not need to be ashamed, handling accurately the word of truth"* (2 Timothy 2:15). If we are not careful, our desire for God's will to be a particular thing may subtly corrupt the interpretation process, and we may read our own ideas into the Scriptures.

Not long ago I was looking back through an old journal from my college days and was reminded of this principle. At the time I was dating a young lady and really wanted the relationship to lead to marriage. As I read the Bible, I had found some Scriptures that seemed to support my desire and began to build my hope around them. I used these verses to convince myself that she was my future mate. Later, when God led me to break up with her and made it clear she was not to be my wife, I saw that I had read into those Scriptures what I wanted to see. I had not interpreted them in the light of their context, but in light of my desires.

I learned the hard way that God does not speak to us from His Word like an Ouija board. An interpretation that discounts and violates a verse's meaning in its context is a wrong interpretation. This is not *"handling accurately the word of truth"* (2 Timothy 2:15). Bible verses are a lot like prisoners of war—if you torture them long enough you can get them to say almost anything you want them to say..

Another danger in applying this principle is **not getting a balanced view of Scripture.** No one verse or passage stands by itself, but each must be interpreted in light of the whole. Again, the counsel of others will help guard against error.

📖 Look at Acts 17:11 again. What did the Bereans do to make sure Paul's message was true?

_____

_____

_____

_____

_____

> *Bible verses are a lot like prisoners of war—if you torture them long enough you can get them to say almost anything you want them to say.*

We must *"examine the Scriptures,"* not just grab a verse and run with it. Everything Paul said, they checked out. They kept going back to the Word to be sure.

It almost goes without saying, but a final way we can miss the boat is that once we discern what God's Word is telling us, we still must make that choice to obey. Steve had direction, but he still had to choose to follow it. Fortunately, God's Word helps us at this point as well. In Psalm 40:8 King David shares an important truth: "I delight to do Thy will, O my God; Thy Law is within my heart." In other words, not only does Scripture show us what God wants us to do, but being in the Word also creates in us a desire to obey what He says.

📖 Look at James 1:22. What is the result for one who hears the Word but does not obey it?

_____

_____

_____

_____

_____

_____

> **"I delight to do Thy will, O my God; Thy Law is within my heart."**
> **—Psalm 40:8**

It is not enough to know what truth is. We must act on that truth or it will not benefit us. Worse, truth without application becomes a deluding influence in our lives. It deceives us into thinking we are spiritual because of how much we know instead of how we live.

FOR ME TO HEAR GOD

HEADLIGHTS SIGN
Day Five
ILLUMINATION OF SCRIPTURE
TURN ON HEADLIGHTS

The Word of God and the will of God are woven together. The Scriptures are His revealed will in so many ways. They are His revealed direction giving light to our path. Imagine how different it is for us compared to men like Abraham and Noah who had no Scriptures to which to refer. We do not have to walk through life blindly. But if the Scriptures are going to benefit us in hearing God, we must understand how they speak. We must see the different ways they address our need—through principles, promises, prohibitions, and proclamations. And we must make sure we handle the Word accurately, not twisting it to say what we want it to say, but letting it speak for itself. Let's look toward applying Scripture to our decision-making.

One of the tools that can help us apply the Word to our need is a topical Bible. The most popular one is *Nave's Topical Bible*. You can find one at your local Christian bookstore, or perhaps borrow one from a friend or pastor. You can be led to particular Scriptures that speak to your need by looking under the topics that relate to your need. For example, Steve could look under "marriage" and find a number of passages listed.

APPLY What are some passages you found that speak to your need?

Passage #1:
Its message:

_____

_____

_____

_____

_____

_____

_____

Passage #2:
Its message:

_____

_____

_____

_____

_____

Another tool that can help you apply the Word to your need is a concordance. The term **exhaustive concordance** means that it will show you every single verse in the Bible that uses a particular word. There are several good ones available both in bound-book form and through computer software. You need to be sure you have one that fits the translation of Scripture you are using. Then you must select a key word that relates to your area of need. For example, Steve could look up the word "marriage" or "husband" or "wife." It may take some time to filter through all the verses, and not every one of them will give you something helpful, but if you'll put forth the effort, it'll be worth it.

APPLY List some passages you found in a concordance that speak to your need.

Passage #3:
Its message:

_____

_____

_____

_____

_____

_____

_____

Passage #4:
Its message:

_____

_____

_____

_____

_____

_____

*Note: If you are unable to locate adequate passages of Scripture at this point, don't worry. More will surface through counsel with others, and you can come back and include these as they do.

Why not close out this week's lesson by taking what you have learned to the Lord. Express your heart and what you intend to do with what you have learned in a written prayer to the Lord.

_____

_____

_____

_____

_____

_____

_____

_____

_____

_____

Notes

THE INFORMATION SIGN:
Wise Counsel

Rich breathed a sigh of relief as he wrote out his resignation notice. He had hated his job from day one, but the money had been good, and with a baby on the way they would soon be losing his wife's income. Rich had initially thought that he could do the job, even though he knew it wasn't the sort of work he enjoyed. But after three months of always being tired and grouchy, of always dreading to go to work, of hating the demands his boss made on him, Rich had had enough. No job, he reasoned, was worth what he was going through, no matter how bad they needed the money. Besides, he had an idea.

Rich had always enjoyed building things. In fact, the country-style woodworking items he made in his basement were very popular among their friends. More than one of them said he could earn a living with such fine wood crafting. "Barbara, I'm going to do it!" he exclaimed with enthusiasm as he shared his idea with his wife. "I'm quitting my job, and I'm going to start a woodworking business in the basement. I can be my own boss and work my own hours, and I'll even be home to watch the baby when you need to go out!"

"The way of a fool is right in his own eyes, but a wise man is he who listens to counsel."

Proverbs 12:15

Like water on a wood fire, the look on Barbara's face dampened his enthusiasm. Even before she exploded in anger that turned to tears, he knew her enough to read the fearful look in her eyes. When the emotions subsided, they talked long and hard about Rich's idea. Barbara knew the factory job had been tough on him. "But what if your idea doesn't work?" she pleaded. "How will we get by with me not working? How will we pay the mortgage? Would you talk with elder Robins first . . . before you do anything?" she asked.

Rich was confused. He had been so confident this was the answer to their problems, but now he wasn't so sure. "What should I do, Lord?" he entreated silently as he laid his resignation aside.

The next signpost we encounter on the road to God's will is the **INFORMATION** sign. It is divinely designed to remind us that we don't always know all the answers, and sometimes we need to ask directions. I am notorious for getting lost when I take my family on vacation trips, yet I hesitate to stop and ask directions. I am sure many of you can relate to this dilemma. It takes so little time to stop and ask directions, but pride keeps prodding us to try to figure it out on our own.

Unfortunately, this same phenomenon shows itself in our spiritual lives. Often as we seek to find God's will, we fail to draw upon the maturity and wisdom of our friends in the body of Christ. Yet clearly God desires that we do this. This doesn't mean that every time we don't know what to do we drop the burden in someone else's lap, nor does it necessarily mean that we should seek counsel from a professional. Any Christian who is mature and knows the Word of God should be able to counsel other believers he knows. What we are talking about here is advice, and that was what Rich needed before making such an important decision.

INFORMATION SIGN

Day One

WISE COUNSEL

How Counsel Can Help

One way counsel can benefit us is to help us find objectivity. When we are in the middle of a circumstance and are trying to discern God's will, it is often hard to be objective. Our emotions and desires can flavor even our most sincere efforts. Someone who isn't wrapped up in the process or bound by its consequences can look at things more easily and with objectivity. Rich needed to realize that his desire to leave a bad working situation could cloud his objectivity and move him to a decision he might later regret.

📖 Read Proverbs 12:15 and write what you learn about counsel.

_____

_____

_____

_____

_____

_____

_____

Proverbs 12:15 tells us, *"The way of a fool is right in his own eyes, but a wise man is he who listens to counsel."* In other words, we need to recognize our ability to deceive ourselves and be willing to listen to those around us.

📖 Look at Proverbs 15:22 and summarize its message.

_____

_____

_____

_____

_____

Another way advice can help us to find God's will is through shared wisdom, insight, and experience. One person cannot hope to be adequately informed on everything. So it is essential that we pool our resources with those around us. Proverbs 15:22 puts it this way: *"Without consultation, plans are frustrated, but with many counselors they succeed."*

No believer, regardless of maturity, is immune to this need for occasional counsel. We do not have to look far in the Scriptures to see the principle illustrated.

📖 Read 2 Samuel 24:1–15 and answer the questions that follow.

What is the action that David initiates (verse 2)?

_____

_____

_____

What is the counsel of David's right hand man (verse 3)?

_____

_____

_____

What does David do with Joab's counsel (verse 4)?

_____

_____

_____

What is the result of David's choice (verse 15)?

_____

_____

_____

In 2 Samuel 24 we read of David's sinful decision to take a census of the people. David's implied purpose for this census was to see how big an army he could put together for battle, indicating his trust in numbers rather than in God. Joab, the commander of the army, counseled David against the move.

> **"Without consultation, plans are frustrated, but with many counselors they succeed."**
>
> **Proverbs 15:22**

Put Yourself in Their Shoes
JOAB

Joab served David loyally, both in political and private relations, throughout his reign. During the Ammonite war it was Joab who aided David in the death of Uriah the Hittite (2 Samuel 11:14–25). Joab helped David's son, Absalom, return after he avenged his sister's rape by Amnon (2 Samuel 14). When Absalom revolted, Joab's former closeness to the prince did not stain his loyalty to David. He followed Absalom beyond the Jordan, and in the final battle of Ephraim, in spite of David's call to spare him and when no one else had courage to act, he killed the prince (2 Samuel 18:2, 11–15). When David decided to conduct a census, Joab tried to persuade him otherwise. Unsuccessful in this, Joab performed the task slowly in order to give the king an opportunity to reconsider the matter (24:1–9).

Who are the "Joabs" around you—the faithful friends whom you can trust for counsel?

However, David refused to listen to Joab; neither did he seek counsel elsewhere. We don't have to wonder if David's choice was wrong. We have his own commentary that he had sinned.

The consequences of David's lack of consultation were great. Although God had provided His guidance and the knowledge of His will through the counsel He placed around David, David's refusal to listen made him susceptible to error. As a result, **seventy thousand men died** in the ensuing plague.

Even though David was a mature believer, a man after God's own heart, he was still capable of mistakes in judgment. Each of us shares that same potential. That is why God places us in a body with relationships of accountability and encouragement.

A PARALLEL PRINCIPLE

📖 Read Deuteronomy 19:15, summarizing its message, and write your thoughts on how it might apply to obtaining counsel.

_____

_____

_____

_____

_____

_____

_____

_____

To guard against false leading, we need to apply the principle of "two or three witnesses," and we should wait for God to begin lining up signposts so as not to draw a conclusion from only one source.

A principle that parallels this concept of counsel is found in the Jewish legal system. The long-cherished principle of American justice that one is "innocent until proven guilty" is based on Jewish legal guidelines which state: *"By the mouth of two or three witnesses every fact may be confirmed"* (Deuteronomy 19:15; Matthew 18:16). In other words, a person is innocent until an allegation is confirmed by two or more independent witnesses. This method guards against false accusations.

So how does this relate to God's will? It is my conviction that we should not base a conclusion about God's will or leading from only one area. Although God does give us leading through His peace, because of the danger of misinterpretation it is unwise to draw a conclusion based only on God's peace. The same holds true for any of the signposts to God's will. To guard against false leading, we need to apply the principle of "two or three witnesses," and we should wait for God to begin lining up signposts so as not to draw a conclusion from only one source.

The wise thing for Rich to do was to seek counsel, and even more, to listen to the counsel he had already received from his wife. Even though I don't always listen to her as quickly as I should, I have learned that God often speaks wisdom to me through my wife. Even when I don't follow her advice, I benefit by taking the time to understand what she is saying.

📖 Look at the verses below and write down your thoughts.

Proverbs 1:5

_____

_____

_____

_____

Proverbs 9:9

_____

_____

_____

_____

The message of Proverbs 1:5 is that it is a wise man who is able to profit from the counsel he is given. A second point, equally important, is that a *"man of understanding"* will not only listen to counsel, but will acquire it. In other words, he will seek it out. Proverbs 9:9 reiterates this idea that it is a wise man who is bettered by counsel.

The Criteria for Counselors

INFORMATION SIGN
Day Three
WISE COUNSEL

No one can be an expert on everything, and in fact, you could well say that even the smartest person is an idiot at something. That means we all need counsel. Our decisions will not be the best they could be if we rely only on our own personal wisdom. Remember, *"the way of a fool is right in his own eyes"* (Proverbs 12:15).

One of the most dismal reigns of Israel's kings belonged to Solomon's son, Rehoboam. It was largely because of Rehoboam's folly that the kingdom of Israel split while he was king.

📖 Look at 2 Chronicles 10:1–8 and write what you learn about Rehoboam's mistakes in choosing and listening to counsel.

_____

_____

_____

_____

_____

When Solomon died, his son Rehoboam consulted with the elders who had served his father. He asked their advice on how he should rule the people.

Did You Know?
REHOBOAM

Rehoboam, Solomon's son, reigned from 931 B.C. to 913 B.C., although only over the "Southern Kingdom" of Judah. Almost immediately after he took the throne, Jeroboam, Solomon's slavemaster, led a revolt that was joined by the ten northern tribes of Israel. Rehoboam's foolish choice to be hard on the people resulted in Israel becoming a divided kingdom. The "Northern Kingdom" of Israel (10 tribes) lasted until 722 B.C. when it was conquered by Assyria. The Southern Kingdom (Judah and Benjamin) lasted until 586 B.C. when it was conquered by Babylon.

He seemingly started out on the right track. But once he had received this wise counsel, he dismissed it. He later forsook the counsel of Solomon's wise men in favor of his buddies—the young men he grew up with. The result was disasterous for him and for Israel.

📖 Now lets look at the reign of Joash. Read 2 Chronicles 24:1–2. What impact did the priest Jehoiada have on Joash's reign?

_____

_____

_____

_____

It seems quite obvious that Jehoiada the priest was a huge factor as to why Joash did right in the sight of the Lord. With Jehoiada at his side as his counselor, Joash made good choices. We learn in this same chapter that Joash led in repairing the temple that had been neglected for years.

📖 Look at 2 Chronicles 24:15–19. What was Joash's reign like after Jehoiada died?

_____

_____

_____

_____

_____

Once his good and godly counselor, Jehoiada, was dead, Joash was not nearly the king he was before. He listened to corrupt counselors who led him astray. Idol worship experienced a resurgence in the latter years of his reign. In fact, he died at the hands of his servants because of his wicked deeds, and was not even buried in the tombs of the kings because of his dishonor.

Good counsel often results in good decisions, just like poor counsel often results in poor decisions.

By now you may be asking yourself questions like "How do I find good counsel?" "From whom should I seek counsel?" "What criteria should I use in seeking counsel?" Finding good counsel involves many factors, and it is important that before you talk to people, you decide where and how to receive the counsel. Let's look at some Scriptural principles.

In varying degrees, below is a list of criteria I use for determining what to seek in a counselor. They are not listed in order of priority or of value.

A COUNSELOR SHOULD POSSESS ONE OR MORE OF THE FOLLOWING TRAITS:

✓ **spiritual and personal maturity**—wisdom

✓ **a commitment to the will of God**

✓ **familiarity with the person to whom he or she is giving advice**—In other words, seek counsel from those close to you. This type of counsel may come from a family member (parent, grandparent, sibling, etc.), or it may simply come from someone familiar with your particular situation (e.g., for marriage counsel look to someone who does that type of counseling).

Put Yourself in Their Shoes

JOASH

Joash reigned over the Southern Kingdom of Judah from 835 B.C. to 796 B.C. Most of his reign was honoring to God, but after the death of the godly priest, Jehoiada, Joash was swayed by the counsel of corrupt leaders from Judah, and ushered back in some of the pagan forms of worship of the Canaanites, most prominently, the worship of the Asherim, which were wooden symbols of a female deity thought to be the mother of some seventy gods.

- ✓ **objectivity**—Seek advice from those who have nothing to gain or lose by your decision. For example, someone who will get the commission from the sale will not provide the best counsel for buying a car.
- ✓ **respectability**—Seek advice from people you respect.
- ✓ **a willingness to listen**—(a non-negotiable)

I don't necessarily look for people who perfectly fit all the above categories, but rather, for different people who fit a few of them exceptionally well. For example, one counselor might know me very well and have a good degree of personal maturity but may not be as spiritually minded as others. That person could still offer valuable input. Another might have great spiritual depth but not know me as well. The key is balance. Don't make all your counselors fit the same mold. The key to obtaining counsel is not in listening to what the counselor has to say, but in listening to what God might say to you through the counselors. His is the most important voice to hear.

BARRIERS TO OBEYING THIS SIGN

INFORMATION SIGN
Day Four
WISE COUNSEL

As with each of the signposts we are considering, there is the potential of misinterpreting the **INFORMATION SIGN.** The most common methods of mistake in this area are (a) selecting the wrong counselors, (b) not listening to them, and (c) leaning more on human counsel than on what God has to say.

First, realize that the counsel is only as good as the counselor. That is why it is essential that you determine criteria for seeking counsel. One common danger is **our tendency to seek counselors who will tell us what we want to hear.** I've found that my critics often make good counselors if I can listen to them without "taking it personally." They help me see a side I don't naturally see. Be sure the person you select is suited to advise in your situation. A single person may not have as much wisdom to offer in a marriage decision as someone who is married. Be choosy in picking your advisors.

📖 Look at 2 Timothy 4:1–3. What does this passage teach us will be a problem for believers seeking counsel in the last days?

_____

_____

_____

_____

Paul is advising Timothy here to make sure he preaches the Word. He warns Timothy that there will be a time when believers won't want to hear truth, but will *"accumulate for themselves teachers in accordance to their own desires."* They will want to have their ears "tickled." In other words, they will want people who will tell them what feels good instead of what is true. I used to get mad at the "doo dah's" on TV who were teaching heresy, until one day it dawned on me that the only reason they could be on TV was that there were people writing checks who wanted to hear them. We must be on guard from seeking counselors who will tell us what we want to hear.

> **The key to obtaining counsel is not in listening to what the counselor has to say, but in listening to what God might say to you through the counselors. His is the most important voice to hear.**

Doctrine
MAJORITY RULE

Although we value democracy, the Christian life is not based on majority rule. In Scripture there are two main examples of majority rule, and both are negative examples. In the Old Testament we see the twelve spies spying out Canaan. The majority (ten spies) said *"There are giants in the land"* and dissuaded Israel from obeying the Lord. It was the minority report (Caleb and Joshua) which held the heart of God. In the New Testament, when Paul was sailing for Italy (Acts 27), he tried to encourage the captain of the ship to put into port for winter, but *"the majority reached a decision to put out to sea from there"* (Acts 27:12). The result was shipwreck.

Doctrine
UNANIMOUS RULE

Conversely, the biblical alternative to majority rule is **unanimity.** Speaking about the Jerusalem church, Acts 15:25 illustrates how the elders there reached a decision: *"having become of one mind. . . ."* The elders of that church operated on the principle of unanimity.

The second danger is **not listening to the counsel we receive.** Don't bother going through the process if you aren't willing to let God speak to you through others. Often we don't mind hearing what others think, but in our heart we've already decided what we want to do. This may have been the case with Solomon's son, Rehoboam.

📖 Look at Proverbs 1:24–33 and write down all of the consequences this passage lists for ignoring wise counsel.

_____

_____

_____

_____

Look at the results: calamity (verse 26), dread (verse 26), distress and anguish (verse 27), lack of truth (verse 28). Those who do not listen to counsel will reap the consequences of their choices (verse 31). They will be destroyed by their own way (verse 32). What a contrast we find in verse 33 for those who do listen to wise counsel—they live securely and are at ease from the dread of evil.

A third danger is **letting the majority rule.** This may be the American way, but it isn't God's way. A classic example is the men who spied out Canaan. Remember that just before they were to enter the promised land, Moses sent twelve spies to look over the land of Canaan.

📖 Read Numbers 13:25–33. What was the majority report and the minority report, and which was the heart of God?

_____

_____

_____

_____

The majority begged the Israelites not to enter this promised land, and the people listened to them. However, it was the minority (Joshua and Caleb) who had God's heart. A majority isn't always right. Because the Israelites followed the majority report, they suffered through forty years of wandering in the wilderness.

The church in which I presently minister is ruled by a council of elders, and major decisions require a unanimous vote. On several occasions I have been held in check by the reservations of just one elder—only later to be glad I did not proceed.

The final potential problem with the **INFORMATION** signpost is that we may tend to **lean more on human counsel than on God.**

📖 Look at Acts 4:13–20. What was the response of Peter and John to the counsel of the Pharisees?

_____

_____

_____

What a model for all of us we find here in the examples of Peter and John. These two men realized that the most important person to please was God. As with each signpost, don't make this one principle regarding counsel stand by itself. Listen to counsel but, most important, listen to God. Sometimes what God says is the opposite of what the counselor says. The key issue with counsel is not just listening to it, but also hearing what God might be saying through that counselor.

I remember some advice given to me a number of years ago by one well-meaning pastor. I was attempting to plant a new ministry on a largely-commuter college campus near our ministry base, and I was having my doubts. It was a tough place to build a ministry. Most of the students lived at home and had part-time jobs. In a meeting with some key pastors in the town to see what could be done, one chided, "That campus chews up Christian workers and spits them out every year. What makes you think you'll be able to plant a ministry there?"

Rather than dissuading me as the advice was intended to do, his message became a motivator to me. It was as if the Lord were saying, "Eddie, when the ministry is built, I can get all the glory," and I was reminded that *"nothing will be impossible with God"* (Luke 1:37). A couple of years ago I was invited back to speak to the weekly meeting of this ministry. Some two hundred college students were coming weekly to hear God's word. To this day, the ministry on this campus continues to thrive as it reaches people for Christ. As I spoke to God's servants on this campus, I remembered that pastor's words and I marveled at the greatness of my God.

❖   ❖   ❖   ❖   ❖   ❖   ❖   ❖   ❖

"Mr. Robins, as a businessman what do you think about my idea?" Rich asked. It was a few days later, and he had acted on Barbara's advice. He met with Bill Robins, one of the elders at their church and a very successful business entrepreneur.

"Well, Rich," Mr. Robins confided, "it sounds to me like your idea has a lot of potential, but you need to realize the odds are stacked against you. Most new businesses don't make it.

"You see, just having a good product is no guarantee of success in the business world. You have to drum up sales, keep your overhead down through wise purchases and good business decisions, and know when to expand and how. Building a successful business that can support you is a complicated task.

"My advice to you," Mr. Robins concluded, "is, don't quit your job until your business begins to show that it can survive. Work at it on the side as long as you can. As your business grows, you'll be able to pick up the business sense to keep it going without the risk of losing your shirt and letting down your family. Businesses that take the time to build up some capital and develop their clientele before trying to carry the burden of supporting you are a lot more likely to make it. Yet even if it never develops to a point of supporting you, at least it should give you a good supplemental income."

In the lean months ahead as Rich built his business, he was glad he waited a while before quitting his job.

"And when they had summoned them, they commanded them not to speak or teach at all in the name of Jesus. But Peter and John answered and said to them, 'Whether it is right in the sight of God to give heed to you rather than to God, you be the judge.'"

Acts 4:18–19

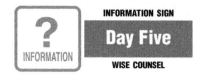
The most important thing we can see in Scripture is not __how__ God spoke, but __that__ God spoke, and that when He did, whomever He was speaking to knew it was God who spoke.

FOR ME TO HEAR GOD

In the decisions of our lives, obtaining counsel means that we are multiplying the wisdom available for the decision. More importantly, it means we are multiplying the ears to hear God. The key is that we are listening to what God might be saying through counsel. How does God speak? There is no standard method when you look at Scripture. Sometimes He spoke from a cloud, and sometimes from a burning bush (Exodus 3). Sometimes He spoke through a wet fleece and sometimes through a dry one (Judges 6). Sometimes He spoke from the mouth of a donkey (Numbers 22:21–33) or a blinding light (Acts 9:3–4), yet other times through *"a still, small voice"* (1 Kings 19:12 KJV). Over and over in the Old and New Testament the method changed, but two things remained constant: **1)** God spoke, and **2)** whomever He was speaking to knew it was God. Jesus said, *"My sheep hear My voice"* (John 10:27). When we hear counsel, we must listen for Him.

APPLY Can you think of a time when God used a counselor to give you good advice?

_____

_____

_____

_____

Can you think of a time when you failed to listen to counsel?

_____

_____

_____

What were the consequences?

_____

_____

_____

APPLY Take a look at the criteria I listed for counselors (pp. 46–47) and begin thinking of whom you can look to for advice. Jot down the names of two or three people who fit several of these criteria.

1. _____

_____

2. _____

_____

3. _____

_____

Once you have selected your counsel, record their directions in the space provided.

COUNSEL #1
Advice:

_____

_____

_____

_____

_____

_____

_____

_____

COUNSEL #2
Advice:

_____

_____

_____

_____

_____

_____

_____

_____

COUNSEL #3
Advice:

_____

_____

_____

_____

_____

_____

COUNSEL #4
Advice:

_____

_____

_____

_____

_____

_____

_____

Take a few minutes to close out what you have learned in this lesson by writing a prayer to the Lord.

_____

_____

_____

_____

_____

_____

_____

_____

_____

_____

Notes

Notes

THE WEIGH STATION SIGN:
Counting the Cost

Nothing is quite so unnerving as the unexpected scream of a five-year-old from directly behind your head after you have been driving for three hours. Our toddler was reaching in both directions from his car seat in the middle of our back seat and was pulling both his brother's and his sister's hair. I was tempted to pull out mine. Somewhere along about the thirteenth time this happened, my resolve weakened, and I agreed with my wife that it was time to get a larger car. The compact station wagon had served us well and had been a dependable car through the past six years and 100,000 plus miles. However, this family of five definitely needed to catch up with the times, and we began looking at the possibility of buying a used minivan.

"Which one should we buy?" became a frequent topic of discussion at the Rasnake household. As I delved into the decision-making process, I quickly learned that buying a car involves more than just a simple choice. It is a myriad of little choices. What color? What size? Do we want a luggage rack? Power windows? Cruise control? Sun roof? Do we want a cassette player or just an AM/FM radio? Air bags or air horns? Vinyl or carpeted floor mats? Is undercoat rust protection important? Do we want an extended warranty? Do we pocket the rebate, or get 2.9-percent financing from the dealer, or do we go to the bank and borrow the money? How does our faith in Christ help us handle this?

Does our faith in Christ help us handle nonspiritual decisions?

You may wonder what all this has to do with God's will, or if I really believe God cares if we get a red Chrysler or a blue Ford. The truth is, many Christians make a big mistake when they divorce such decisions from the wisdom God has to offer. No, God will not write in the sky: "Buy the blue one, and don't forget cruise control." However, He has given some principles in Scripture that help us in managing the finances He provides.

THE PRINCIPLE ILLUSTRATED

The next signpost we encounter on the road to God's will is the **WEIGH STATION** sign. Often, as we travel on our highways, we see trucks lined up at these stations to weigh in. This sign reminds us of the need to weigh our options carefully as we make decisions. We must count the cost ahead of time. To make a good decision, we need to do some homework. We need to find out as much as we can about every aspect of the choice to be made. To a degree, our final decision is only as good as the information we base it on.

Jesus emphasized this principle in Luke 14 as He explained His challenging statement, *"Whoever does not carry his own cross and come after Me cannot be My disciple"* (verse 27). To illustrate, Jesus related two hypothetical situations.

Look at Luke 14:28–30 and answer the questions below.

What are the circumstances of Jesus' illustration here?

_____

_____

_____

What were the consequences of not counting the cost?

_____

_____

_____

First, Jesus said:

> *"Which one of you, when he wants to build a tower, does not first sit down and calculate the cost, to see if he has enough to complete it? Otherwise, when he has laid a foundation, and is not able to finish, all who observe it begin to ridicule him, saying, 'This man began to build and was not able to finish.'"* (Luke 14:28–30)

This story creates a graphic mental picture of the necessity of counting the cost. A man begins a construction project, but because of poor planning, he is unable to finish it. In my mind I can visualize a half-built tower with weeds growing up in the center. The mortar is crumbling in places and stones lay scattered on the ground. Strangers gawk as they pass by, and neighbors share a knowing smirk as they look at it, a monument to not counting the cost. I know what that feels like all too well. Our last car was a good one, but soon after I bought it, I learned I could have gotten the same

> "Which one of you, when he wants to build a tower, does not first sit down and calculate the cost, to see if he has enough to complete it?"
>
> Luke 14:28

car with the same features for about $1,500 less. I thought about that every month when I made the payment, and that fact motivates me to do my homework.

As if for double emphasis, Jesus related a second illustration. Look at Luke 14:31–32 and answer the questions below.

What are the circumstances of Jesus' illustration here?

_____

_____

_____

What were the consequences of not counting the cost?

_____

_____

_____

_____

Jesus continues:

> *"Or what king, when he sets out to meet another king in battle, will not first sit down and take counsel whether he is strong enough with ten thousand men to encounter the one coming against him with twenty thousand? Or else, while the other is still far away, he sends a delegation and asks for terms of peace"* (Luke 14:31–32).

In this situation, a king must count the cost of waging war or surrender. Not counting the cost could result in needless death or enslavement.

📖 It may very well be that Christ drew both of these hypothetical illustrations from Proverbs 20:18. Read the verse and compare it to Luke 14.

_____

_____

_____

_____

_____

> **"Prepare plans by consultation, and make war by wise guidance."**
>
> **Proverbs 20:18**

Proverbs 20:18 states, *"Prepare plans by consultation, and make war by wise guidance."* As the two illustrations in Luke 14 allude to construction and military strategy, Proverbs 20:18 does likewise. Getting advice and counsel from others, as discussed in the previous lesson, is a significant factor in counting the cost.

DIFFERENT KINDS OF DECISIONS

One might argue that the **WEIGH STATION** signpost, which symbolizes our need to "count the cost" isn't really a separate signpost but the application of all of other signposts. I chose to separate it for

WEIGH STATION SIGN
Day Two
COUNTING THE COST

two reasons: **(1)** for emphasis, and **(2)** because it teaches us that different questions sometimes require different processes.

📖 Look again at Luke 14:28–30 and answer the questions below.

What kind of decision is being made here, and what deadline is faced?

_____

_____

_____

_____

_____

What will happen if nothing is decided?

_____

_____

_____

_____

Jesus' illustrations offer two different kinds of questions, each requiring a different process:

1) Whether-to-or-not
2) Either-or

With the first illustration, the building of a tower, Jesus shows how our principle applies in a whether-to-or-not decision: "Should I build a tower?" In Jesus' illustration of the tower, there is no particular deadline to the decision. It would be okay if no decision were made. The project would simply remain on hold. No harm would be done by waiting.

📖 Look again at Luke 14:31–32 and answer the questions below.

What kind of decision is being made here, and what deadline is faced?

_____

_____

_____

_____

_____

What will happen if nothing is decided?

_____

_____

_____

_____

_____

In this second illustration, Jesus builds on the decision-making idea pointing to an "either-or" decision. In a "whether-to-or-not" decision, as in Jesus' tower illustration, it really does no damage if no decision is reached. With the second illustration, however, some decision had to be made. The implication is that the king realized, after counting the cost, that fighting might be futile, so he pursued an alternative: to seek acceptable peace terms. If the king made no decision, the decision for war would be made for him.

I like this second illustration. As the king tried to determine the strength of his army, his steps show the process of counting the cost. Reading between the lines, it would seem he was not only identifying their numerical strength but also their valor. He asks himself, "Are my ten thousand valiant enough to tackle his twenty thousand?" Notice there is no answer, no indication of a decision. Perhaps it is too close to call, so he investigates his other options. He sends a delegation to the approaching king to see what the terms of surrender would be. Notice the time factor, too. He sends his inquiry *"while the other is still far away."* He doesn't wait until the last minute.

We can learn much about counting the cost from these words of Christ. Applying some of these principles to buying a vehicle meant going to the library and reading up on safety records and consumer reports. It meant praying over our family budget to see what we could afford and how that would affect our freedom to give to the Lord's work. It meant test drives and shopping around. Homework isn't always easy, but neither is living with the consequences of an unwise choice.

Learning How to Count the Cost

WEIGH STATION SIGN

Day Three

COUNTING THE COST

Certainly, we would consider someone foolish who undertook a building project without first determining if he could afford to finish it. Likewise, we would have little sympathy for a king who goes to war without adequate forethought. Yet so often we fail to apply this principle in areas of our own life. We make purchases that blow our budget. We say yes to projects we don't have time to complete. We make spur-of-the-moment decisions we later regret. None of us is immune from error. Cultivating the habit of counting the cost will help us avoid these common miscalculations.

📖 The process of counting the cost involves several steps. As we look at Christ's message in Luke 14:27–30, we can identify many of them. Look at the passage again and see what the first step was in both situations.

_____

_____

_____

_____

_____

_____

Doing your homework is not always easy, but neither is living with the consequences of an unwise choice.

Principle #1—Identify the Needs

In both of Christ's illustrations we see that the first step in counting the cost is to identify the needs presented. In the case of the tower, the builder must *"sit down and calculate the cost."* Alfred Plummer, in his *Critical and Exegetical Commentary on the Gospel According to St. Luke* (Fortress, 1901), points out that the phrase *"sit down"* represents "long and serious consideration," not just idle thought. Of course this consideration would apply to finances—estimating how much the materials and hired manpower would cost. It would also apply to time: how much time the builder would have to put in personally and how long the project would take.

The king going into battle would have to determine the size and strength of the opposition. How many soldiers do they have? How many horses or camels will they bring? Do you see the principle? The first step we undertake should be to clearly understand the need.

📖 Now, look at Christ's message in Luke 14:27–30 again. What was the second step in both situations?

_____

_____

_____

_____

_____

Word Study

"TO BUILD A TOWER"

Púrgos (Gr., *tower*)—This particular word was normally used of a wall built for defense as in the wall of a city or the watchtower of a vineyard. This same word appears in Luke 13:4, where it refers to a portion of a city wall.

Principle #2—Identify the Resources

As we study Christ's explanation, the next step we see is to identify and inventory the relevant resources at our disposal. For the man building a tower, the resources would be his finances, his servants and workers, and his raw materials. How much money could he afford to spend? How many presently on his payroll could he involve in the task, and how many could be hired? How much of the needed materials (trees, stone, etc.) does he already have?

For the king going into battle, the resources would be the manpower and military equipment available to him. His determination would need to be both qualitative and quantitative.

📖 The example of the king going into battle presents us with two additional principles. Read that part of the story again and see if you can identify them.

_____

_____

_____

_____

The two additional principles are: **factoring in time;** and, **evaluating other options.** The king, in a timely manner, might determine what the other army expected for a peace treaty.

Principle #3—Factoring Time

To factor in time requires adequate forethought. Don't wait to start making a decision until it has to be made. Procrastination opens us up to hasty and sometimes unwise decisions, especially when no time is designated for counting costs. We must plan to plan. We must gather information and evaluate it before the deadline.

In college I was notorious for putting off writing papers until the last minute. I had convinced myself that the pressure helped me. In reality, however, I often found myself writing without time to do adequate research and with my senses dulled by all-nighters at the typewriter. It took some time for me to realize that the grades I got on such projects didn't adequately reflect my abilities. I was settling for less because I was too lazy to plan ahead.

Don't we often do the same thing in decision-making? Don't we sometimes settle for less than the best because we don't factor in time?

The king mentioned in Christ's example allowed himself adequate time to calculate his strategy by starting his planning early. He also may have bought himself some time by negotiating. By sending a delegation to meet the opposing army, he stalled them. He persuaded them to wait for the process. If this king then decided to fight, he had bought precious time to prepare his defenses. A defensive battle can be waged with fewer men if proper preparations have been made.

So what practical lessons can we glean from this this principle of factoring time? First, we can factor in time by forming our plans early, not waiting till the deadline. Second, we can factor in time by communicating with the person who sets the deadline and allowing him to participate in our information–gathering process. Getting other parties involved in our plans may actually shorten our time requirements. At least it will make deadline setters more sensitive to our needs should it become necessary to allow more time. Involving the deadline setter should not be implemented as a stall tactic but only as a means to ensure that all costs have been counted.

Principle #4—Evaluating Other Options

An additional lesson we can learn from this hypothetical king is the need to evaluate our other options. As we shared in the introduction to this study, **"Beginning the Process"** on "The Binary Trap," rarely do situations present us with only two options. If nothing else, time (waiting) is always a third. The king, rather than limiting himself to either winning or losing the battle, began checking to see if he could come up with some other option. He inquired of the other king as to his terms for peace.

Often in biblical times, such a peace treaty would involve one king subjecting his nation to slavery as well as forfeiture of lands and goods. There is no indication in Christ's example, but we can infer from His scenario that the king would then have to sit down and evaluate the terms for peace to see if they were worth accepting. If the terms for peace were not acceptable, the king would take his troops into battle and pray for God to intervene on their behalf. In some cases a fight to the death would be a better alternative than surrender. Some nations would torture their conquered subjects and rape their women. So the king had much to evaluate, and he would need to do whatever he could to increase his options.

If we desire to make effective decisions, we often will need to create our own options rather than limit ourselves to only those presented to us. Daniel and his three friends did that. The Babylonian authorities placed them in a binary situation. They gave these four young men only two options: either eat from the king's menu and violate God's dietary restrictions, or refuse and face the king's wrath. I'm sure Daniel evaluated the situation and said to himself, "I don't like either choice," so he became creative. He took it upon himself to come up with an alternative that satisfied both camps. Daniel realized the king's goal wasn't really to make him eat the food but to make him as healthy as possible, so he suggested a test to show that God's diet plan would reach that goal better. In the end, everyone came out a winner. That is a worthy goal in negotiation: Try to find a way for everyone to win.

Rarely do situations present us with only two options. Oftentimes, the act of waiting is a viable third option.

BARRIERS TO OBEYING THIS SIGN

One of the realities in decision-making is that more often than not, we don't have as much information as we want—yet the decision still has to be made. Showing faith when decisions need to be made implies we are walking in the Light (Jesus) and trusting that Light is enough to reveal God's purposes.

As with each of our signposts, the potential of misapplication or non-application applies. To avoid this mistake we must consider the dangers. Just as a real **WEIGH STATION** sign on the highway is of no use to a truck driver who refuses to stop at the weigh station, the symbolic weigh station signpost is of no use to a Christian who neglects to count the costs and weigh all options. Oftentimes those of us who do pay heed to the signpost of cost counting are misled in several ways. These ways are the barriers to obeing this signpost

One potential danger is that **counting the cost becomes an excuse for deferring a decision.** We use it to avoid making a final decision. Some of us have a difficult time finalizing a decision. We vacillate and second-guess ourselves silly. If this is true to you, part of the problem may be simply inexperience and a lack of education in biblical decision-making. But it also may be rooted in personality and background. For instance, if you grew up in a family where all your decisions were critiqued by your parents and frequently found wanting by their standards, you may have difficulty trusting your own decisions as an adult. If you tend to be a perfectionist, you may spend too much time counting the cost and trying to come up with a perfect decision. One of the realities of decision-making is that more often than not, we don't have as much information as we want—yet the decision still has to be made. Change in these areas will be slow, but becoming aware of weaknesses is a step in the right direction.

📖 Read Acts 25:23—26:32.

On what charges was Paul being tried?

_____

_____

_____

What was Agrippa's overall impression of Paul's message?

_____

_____

_____

_____

What response did Agrippa make to the opportunity of salvation?

_____

_____

_____

In the course of Paul's many trials for false charges brought against him by the Jews, one such trial brought him before King Agrippa of Palestine. The account Luke gives us in Acts of Paul's testimony before Agrippa is one of the fullest explanations we have of Paul's conversion to Christ. In the end, Agrippa is quite impressed with all Paul has to say, and makes the statement: *"In a short time you will persuade me to become a Christian."* Sadly, Agrippa brought the meeting to a close with no decision, and by delaying a decision for Christ it appears he avoided the decision altogether. There is no indication Agrippa ever converted to Christianity.

Another danger of which we need to be mindful is **making decisions by default.** I saw this many times in my years of ministry with college students. Often, students would not take advantage of an opportunity, such as a conference or a retreat, not because they sought the Lord and decided not to go, but because they put off deciding until it was too late to go. They decided—a negative decision by default. I see the same tendencies in some of the adults I minister to now. Realize this: It is okay and biblically right sometimes to decide to wait, but it is wrong and it is sin to decide by not making a decision.

Another danger when we apply this principle of counting the cost is leaning too heavily on it. The **WEIGH STATION** principle fosters a danger of **making decisions by sight, not faith.** Finances play a role in some decisions, but sometimes even when the finances aren't there, God leads us to do something, and He wants us to trust Him to provide the finances. The same is true of many other aspects of cost-counting decisions. Even when we have counted the cost, we must be willing to make a faith-based decision, not simply a sight-based one.

📖 Look at the passages listed below and answer the corresponding questions.

Exodus 14
What was the "sight" decision?

_____

_____

_____

What was the "faith" decision?

_____

_____

_____

What was the result?

_____

_____

_____

_____

Judges 7
What was the "sight" decision?

_____

_____

_____

_____

Do you make decisions by faith or by sight?

What was the "faith" decision?

_____

_____

_____

What was the result?

_____

_____

_____

We must count the cost, but our calculating scales must make room for God.

When Gideon marched with his army of three hundred, a sight decision would have sent him home instead of into battle. When Moses and Israel had Pharaoh at their backs and the Red Sea in front of them, a sight decision would have said surrender instead of sending them through the sea. In both cases walking by sight would have robbed them of the blessing that came through faith. We see this same reality from the negative side when Israel refused to go into the promised land because there were giants in the land. As a result, they spent forty years wandering in the wilderness. We must count the cost, but our calculating scales must make room for God.

I remember my first year of full-time ministry with college students at the University of Virginia. After one semester, I was convinced that the attitudes of the intellectual and upper-middle-class students and the restrictions of the administration made a movement of impact for Christ unlikely, if not impossible. But God brought me to the point where I realized that no matter how many possibilities for failure I could place on one side of the scale, God was still on the other side of the scale. Years later, the men at UVA through which God allowed me to invest my life are still serving Christ all over the globe. We do need to count the cost, but God must be considered in our counting.

Applying the four **WEIGH STATION** signpost principles proved very helpful to me in buying a vehicle. Shopping around, I discovered that buying hubcaps, floor mats, and a stereo from Kmart instead of the dealer would save me several hundred dollars. *Consumer Reports* magazine taught me that much hidden profit for a car dealer is built into exorbitant mark-up prices for inexpensive services such as underbody rust protection and stainguard treatment for fabric seats. Simple addition and subtraction showed me that discount interest rates from dealers really wouldn't save me money, especially if it meant buying a different car from the one I wanted.

WEIGH STATION SIGN

Day Five

COUNTING THE COST

APPLYING THE PRINCIPLE

What about you? Have you done your homework on the decision you need to make? Expressions like "Better safe than sorry" and "An ounce of prevention is worth a pound of cure" become clichés because they are true. We either will count the cost in advance, and use those calculations to help us in decision-making, or we will count the cost later and use them in our repentance and remorse.

APPLY Think about the dangers with this signpost. Can you think of a time when you or someone you know allowed counting the cost to become an excuse for deferring a decision?

_____

_____

_____

_____

_____

What was the result?

_____

_____

_____

_____

_____

Can you think of a time when you or someone you know made a significant decision by failing to make a decision?

_____

_____

_____

_____

What was the result?

_____

_____

_____

_____

Can you think of a time when you or someone you know made a "sight" decision when you should have made a "faith" decision?

_____

_____

_____

_____

What was the result?

_____

_____

_____

_____

> *"Man is feeble and frail and prone to failing."*
>
> *—Charles Spurgeon*

If we are wise we will learn from the mistakes of others instead of making them ourselves. This is one of the powerful benefits of the narratives we find in Scripture. But sooner or later we will make mistakes of our own, for as the venerable preacher of the nineteenth century, Charles Haddon Spurgeon, once said, "Man is feeble and frail and prone to falling." When we do fail, we must learn from our own mistakes or be doomed to repeating them throughout our lives.

APPLY Use the following structured questions to assist you in counting the cost of your decision:

Identify the Need. In the space below, clarify as near as you can the need or circumstances confronting you.

_____

_____

_____

_____

_____

_____

Identify Your Resources. List as completely as you can the resources you have that bear on this decision.

_____

_____

_____

_____

_____

_____

Factor in Time. How much time do you have to make this decision?

_____

_____

_____

What do you need to do to insure that you have enough time to do a good job?

_____

_____

_____

_____

Options. What are your present options in this decision?

_____

_____

_____

_____

How can you modify these options to make them better suited?

_____

_____

_____

What options can you create to resolve the situation better?

_____

_____

_____

_____

Why not close out this lesson by writing a prayer to the Lord, expressing your heart in application of this week's lesson?

_____

_____

_____

_____

_____

_____

_____

_____

_____

Notes

THE DETOUR SIGN:
Providential Circumstances

"Eddie, I really believe you are the man for the job." These words, coming from an old friend and former pastor, were like music to my ears. I was in the middle of a lengthy and sometimes frustrating process of interviewing for the position of youth pastor at a Baptist church. This church just happened to be the very first church I attended as a new believer, and it was reassuring to hear again that the pastor both wanted me for the job and believed I would get it.

During college, I had received a clear sense from the Lord of a calling towards ministry, but I wasn't certain when or where God would lead me to begin work in this calling. Upon graduation I took a job managing a restaurant. The money was good, especially now that I was engaged and soon to have a wife to support. But the hours were long, and the chances to minister were few and far between. From inside I sensed a deepening longing to give the Lord the best hours of my day in service, not just the leftovers.

When I had heard that my former church was looking for a youth pastor, my heart skipped a beat. God had greatly used the saintly pastor to ground me in the faith. He taught the Scriptures well and had a strong sense of burden for the lost. The thought of working alongside him and learning from him seemed too

"Then Job answered the LORD, and said, 'I know that Thou canst do all things, And that no purpose of Thine can be thwarted.'"

Job 42:1–2

good to be true, but after I met with him, we both knew we wanted it to work out. Now I was going through the interview process with the search committee and was patiently biting my nails as they interviewed others. Not only would this job allow me to get into the ministry full-time, but it would also mean a better salary, good news for a man who had wedding plans.

The church had started with a list of fifteen potential candidates, which quickly narrowed to ten. The pastor frankly shared with me that he considered me at the top of the list. The group was narrowed to five and then to three, and he still believed I was the man for the job. At that point I knew I wanted the position more than I ever wanted it before. Finally the list was narrowed to two men, myself and another, and the pastor affirmed his belief in me.

The committee however was divided. They had committed to make a unanimous decision, but they could not seem to come to agreement. The process had gone on for more than six months with no end in sight, so a deadline was set to resolve this impasse and make a final decision.

I was nervous with excitement as I dialed the phone to learn from the pastor what decision had been made. My wedding was now only a month away, and my wife-to-be and I had found an apartment near the church. In fact, we had already started planning our budget based on the new salary. As soon as the pastor answered, I knew something was wrong. He said, "Eddie, I would never have believed what happened tonight," and he began to explain what I already sensed.

The committee had been deadlocked. Some wanted me for the job, others wanted the other fellow, and none were willing to budge. After hours of deliberation, there seemed no way to come to agreement. Then someone remembered a Bible verse about Judas' replacement being chosen by casting lots (see Acts 1:16–26). Quickly everyone agreed to the plan, and both names were placed into a hat as the committee members prayed for God to use this method to direct them. "Eddie, I really believed your name was going to come out of the hat," the pastor painfully related.

Suddenly my world had shattered.

Perhaps tougher to accept, but no less valid, one of the important signposts we come to on the road to God's will is the **DETOUR** signpost. I encountered a detour sign the other day when I was out driving. At first I thought it was an annoying inconvenience. But when I discovered it had been placed there because of a washed-out bridge, I recognized it served for my protection. I wonder how many times life's detour signs, though frustrating and inconvenient, have served through God's sovereignty to protect me. God speaks through our circumstances, and we can save ourselves much anxiety if we learn to listen to what they say. Are there any **DETOUR** signposts in your life?

Did You Know?

CASTING LOTS

While it is true that the disciples cast lots to determine who should replace Judas among the twelve (see Acts 1:15–26), many theologians do not believe this choice was affirmed by God. They see the apostle Paul as God's choice to be the twelfth man among the apostles. Scripture doesn't tell us for sure. In the Old Testament casting lots was one of the methods the priests used to determine God's will (using the Urim and Thummim), but this account in Acts is the only example we find of the practice in the New Testament.

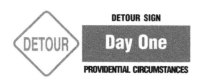

DETOUR SIGN
Day One
PROVIDENTIAL CIRCUMSTANCES

THE DIVINE DESIGN OF DETOURS

What did I learn from my experience? I saw two clear purposes behind God's sovereign working: (1) He wants to **provide** for me; and, (2) He wants to **protect** me. There is no wasted time in the unfolding of God's will. His will has so much to offer; it makes no sense to settle for mine. His will provides the best of everything! Often, in God's gracious sovereignty, He places a detour on my path to put me back on His path. Getting turned down for the youth-pastor position did that for me.

You see, during my last year of college I sensed the Lord leading me to join the staff of Campus Crusade for Christ to have a ministry reaching college students for Him. I said yes, went through the application process, and was accepted on staff. As my time to go through training and begin raising my support neared, I began having second thoughts. "I just didn't have a peace about it," I explained to friends. Truth is, I was fearful of trusting God to raise my support. I wasn't looking forward to months of asking people I didn't know to invest in my ministry.

So when I was offered a restaurant management job, I jumped at the chance for a steady salary, and thus began eighteen months of unhappiness. The story of Jonah graphically illustrates that no one is more miserable than the person running from God's call. Like what the huge fish did for Jonah, a **DETOUR** sign put me back on the path of God's leading.

We see the "detour" principle operating many times in the life of the apostle Paul. In his letter to the believers at Philippi, he addressed their concern over his "detour" to prison, and points them to a different perspective.

Look at Philippians 1:12–14 and answer the questions below.

What do you think the Philippians thought about Paul having to be in prison?

_____

_____

_____

_____

What was Paul's perspective on his imprisonment?

_____

_____

_____

_____

What resulted from Paul's imprisonment?

_____

_____

_____

_____

When Paul writes, *"Now I want you to know, brethren, that my circumstances have turned out for the greater progress of the gospel,"* he makes it clear that he was concerned that they might have a different perspective. They probably thought the cause of Christ was being hindered by what to them appeared to be an obstacle. In fact, the opposite was true. Paul mentions two positive results from his imprisonment: the gospel was being showcased among the

Did You Know?

THE PRAETORIAN GUARD

Situated in Rome, the Praetorium was the quarters built by Tiberius for the imperial bodyguard, known as the "praetorian guard" (Philippians 1:13). This official police force was some 9,000 soldiers strong. Apparently it was through Paul's arrest that all of these soldiers and the related officials of the Roman court heard the gospel. While it took years for many of these seeds to bear fruit, it is worth noting that eventually Christianity became the state religion of the Roman empire.

Praetorian Guard, and the believers were gaining boldness through seeing his example. God's detour provided greater evangelism opportunities for Paul as well as greater faith and boldness for the church at Rome. It also protected him from the deadly intentions of antagonistic Jews whose plot to kill him was thwarted by his arrest. Paul didn't ask to be in prison, but he knew once he got there that God had a higher purpose.

Think for a moment about how many books of the Bible were written by Paul from prison. Name as many as you can recall.

_____

_____

_____

_____

_____

_____

_____

We know that Paul wrote Ephesians, Philippians, Colossians, and Philemon during his first imprisonment. He wrote 2 Timothy during his last imprisonment. Luke records many details of his various arrests and trials in the book of Acts. It is quite possible that other epistles authored by Paul may have been written from jails as well. Many of these "letters from prison" that we treasure might not have been written under different circumstances.

📖 Another detour sign in the Scriptures is seen in the scattering of the early Church. Look at Acts 1:8.

What was Christ's plan for the spreading of the gospel?

_____

_____

_____

_____

_____

SPREADING THE GOSPEL

Many see Acts 1:8 as the outline for the book of Acts. Jesus said, *"You will be my witnesses both in Jerusalem, and in all Judea and Samaria, and even to the remotest part of the earth."* The book of Acts chronologically records the gospel as it spread to each of these areas.

What did it take for the Church to start sharing the gospel outside of Jerusalem?

_____

_____

_____

_____

_____

Christ's last command to the Church at His ascension was to take the gospel to the *"remotest part of the earth"* (Acts 1:8), yet it wasn't until the persecution that began with Stephen that believers began to leave Jerusalem. The persecution served as a catalyst to spread the gospel to the world by spreading believers throughout the world. Because God is sovereign, Satan's attempt to stamp out Christianity turned out for the progress of the gospel, a divinely-designed detour: God took what men meant for evil and used it for good.

WHAT DETOURS LOOK LIKE

God is sovereign. Every event under the heavens is subject to His scrutiny, and nothing escapes His notice. He is not, as some have suggested, a "cosmic clockmaker" who created the universe, wound it up and then sat back to watch it run. Because He is our "Good Shepherd," He is constantly guiding us even though we don't always recognize what He is doing.

📖 Read 1 Corinthians 16:8–9 and answer the questions that follow.

What was Paul's original desire? (look at the context)

_____

_____

_____

What detoured him from going on to Corinth?

_____

_____

_____

God is not, as some have suggested, a "cosmic clockmaker" who created the universe, wound it up, and then sat back to watch it run.

God's detours take many different shapes and sizes. Sometimes, as in Paul's experience in Ephesus (1 Corinthians 16:8–9), God speaks to us through "open doors," divinely-designed opportunities for ministry. Paul apparently planned a trip to Corinth that ended up being delayed because of the ministry success in Ephesus. Not all open doors are God's will, as we will see in a later chapter, but they are always opportunities which must be prayerfully considered.

📖 Look at Acts 16:6–10.

What kept Paul from preaching in the Phrygian and Galatian region?

_____

_____

_____

Why did they not travel into Bithynia?

_____

_____

_____

What happened after the closed door of Bithynia to redirect them?

_____

_____

The "detour" that sent Paul to Macedonia instead of Galatia resulted in the establishment of significant churches such as the ones in Philippi, Thessalonica, Berea, and Corinth. Many of these churches were recipients of letters from Paul that eventually became books of the Bible – Philippians, First and Second Thessalonians, and First and Second Corinthians.

DETOUR SIGN
Day Three
PROVIDENTIAL CIRCUMSTANCES

Sometimes God speaks through open doors. Other times, as in Paul's efforts to take the gospel to Asia and Bithynia (Acts 16:6–7), He speaks through closed doors. We are not told exactly how the Holy Spirit forbid them to preach in Galatia, nor do we know exactly what is meant that the Spirit of Jesus did not permit them to go into Bithynia. The main point however, is clear. It was not until after the closed door of Bithynia that they were redirected to Macedonia, one of Paul's most fruitful mission fields.

My initial decision to decline joining the staff of Campus Crusade for Christ was based on my fear of raising support. Though this fear reflected some weakness of faith, I still wanted to do God's will. The detour sign of not getting the church job put me back on the previous path. Six months later, I did follow the Lord's leading and joined the Campus Crusade staff. It is important to realize that every open door does not constitute a call, and every closed door doesn't mean we give up, but God can and sometimes does speak through such circumstances.

The main point that the **DETOUR** signpost teaches us is that God in His sovereignty may give us detours to get us on the right road. When you think about it, this is truly an encouraging thought. Because God desires even more than we do that we follow His will, He is willing and able to redirect us if we sincerely want to follow Him. Have you ever been divinely redirected like this? I have.

BARRIERS TO OBEYING THE SIGN

As with each of the signposts to God's will, there is the potential of misapplication. If we aren't careful, we might draw the wrong conclusions about what God is saying. As we noted above, **an open door or opportunity doesn't automatically mean God is the one calling.**

📖 Look at Matthew 4:1–10.

What open doors were placed before Jesus, and by whom?

_____

_____

_____

_____

What does this tell us about assuming open doors are God's will?

_____

_____

_____

_____

While it is true that God places open doors before us, and sometimes speaks His will in that way, this does not mean all open doors are from God. Satan also places open doors in our path. When he tempted Jesus in the wilderness, he presented Him with the opportunity to have *"all the kingdoms of the world."* Clearly however, this open door was not God's will.

📖 Read 2 Corinthians 2:12–13 and answer the questions below.

Why had Paul gone to Troas?

_____

_____

_____

What did he find there?

_____

_____

_____

Why didn't he take advantage of this open door?

_____

_____

_____

Sometimes other pressing needs come before an open door. We see this in Paul's second letter to Corinth. Paul had an open door for ministry to Troas, but the Lord led him to pass it up and go to Macedonia to see how the Corinthians were doing. Although the spread of the gospel was central to Paul's life, he was also in the middle of a delicate situation in his mentoring of the Corinthian church, and in this case he determined before the Lord that this mentoring of the Corinthians needed to take precedent.

So how do we know when an open door is God's will? I think the important principle to recognize here is that an open door must be considered carefully. It is God's will that we go to Him about an apparent opportunity instead of dismissing it without prayer. When I am faced with an open door, I seek the Lord about it, and I trust Him to confirm His will with additional signposts. Remember that no single signpost is confirmation by itself.

📖 What does 2 Corinthians 5:7 tell us about the Christian walk?

_____

_____

_____

_____

Another ever-present danger in looking at our circumstances is that **we might interpret them by our feelings instead of by faith.** The Christian life is a faith life. It is lived through moment-by-moment trust in the Lord. Because we walk by faith instead of sight, we cannot trust open and closed doors without praying them through.

A troubling question came from my church job experience: How could I be so sure something was God's will and be so wrong? Perhaps you have made similar misjudgments. We all need to recognize how easily personal desires

Did You Know?
THE LOST EPISTLE

The situation Paul refers to in 2 Corinthians 2:12–13 occurred between the writing of First and Second Corinthians. Apparently Paul wrote an additional letter to the Corinthian church, which has been lost. It contained harsh words concerning their failure to deal with a sinning brother in the church. Paul was awaiting word from Titus who was to bring a report on how the Corinthians responded to Paul's rebuke. We learn from the context of these verses, as well as from 2 Corinthians 7:5–13, that Paul did eventually meet up with Titus and learned of the Corinthian repentance.

> *God is far more concerned with our character than with our circumstances. Circumstances are one of His favorite tools to shape our character.*

can get in the way of understanding clearly what God is saying. My longing to be in the ministry and my love for my former pastor had clouded my interpretation of God's leading. Circumstances can be misinterpreted easily, and our human wants or fleshly desires for comfort may deceive us into seeing something as God's will when it isn't.

Let's face it. No one likes trials. Nobody wants to go through difficult circumstances. I don't particularly like the idea that persecution might be God's will for me. I'd rather stick my head in the sand and naively believe that life is supposed to be easy. However, God is far more concerned with my character than with my circumstances. In fact, circumstances are one of His favorite tools to shape my character. He would like me to learn my lessons academically through studying the Word, but He also lets me learn them vocationally by putting me into situations where I have to apply what the Word says.

If we aren't careful, we will mistake our fleshly desires for ease and comfort for God's leading. It isn't surprising that people buy into wrong doctrines—those teaching that, if we'll just have enough faith, we'll have all the money we want, all the healing we want, everything. We really want those things to be true, but God doesn't fit neatly into our box, and often His use of providential circumstances means difficult times for us.

There is good news in this, though. Because God is sovereign, He is able to turn the difficult times around and cause them to work for our good. Notice I am not saying that God causes bad things to happen to His people. What I am saying is that, because He is sovereign, He can use anything that happens to us to accomplish His will. And when I grumble and complain about my circumstances, in effect, I am accusing God of mismanaging my life.

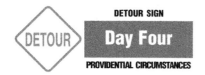

DETOUR SIGN

Day Four

PROVIDENTIAL CIRCUMSTANCES

SOVEREIGNTY AND CIRCUMSTANCE

Consider the story of Joseph, Jacob's son. Genesis chapters 37—45 tell us the story of Joseph and how he ended up in Egypt. His jealous brothers sold him into slavery. Then his master's wife wrongly accused him of attempted rape, and he was thrown into prison. While in prison, he interpreted a dream for one of the king's servants, and eventually interpreted a dream for the king.

Where was God in all of this? Right in the middle. God used these difficult, painful detours to accomplish His will. He turned them around and used Joseph's slavery and prison experience to place him as Prime Minister over all of Egypt. Now that is what I call sovereignty!

📖 The culmination of the story of Joseph is found in Genesis 45 when he finally reveals himself to his brothers. Look at Genesis 45:1–10.

Why wasn't Joseph angry with his brothers, and why did he tell them they shouldn't be angry or grieved with themselves (verse 5)?

_____

_____

Why did Joseph believe he was where he was (verse 7)?

_____

_____

_____

_____

How do you think Joseph could say that it was not his brothers' actions that placed him where he was?

_____

_____

_____

_____

Notice what Joseph learns in all of this. Joseph wasn't angry with his brothers because he recognized that God had a higher purpose. Joseph had absolute confidence that God had put him where he was so that he could save many lives, including his own family. When his brothers come to Joseph again after their father (Jacob) died, they were afraid that he would now seek revenge.

Look at Joseph's response to his brothers in Genesis 50:19–20.

What is the main message of Joseph's response?

_____

_____

_____

_____

What does that say about God's sovereignty?

_____

_____

_____

_____

Joseph, in this passage, makes one of the clearest explanations in Scripture regarding God's sovereignty. He counsels his brothers, _"Do not be afraid, for am I in God's place?"_ In other words, "I am exactly where I ought to be." He continues, _"And as for you, you meant evil against me, but God meant it for good in order to bring about this present result."_ What a powerful thought! Because God is sovereign, He is able to take the evil actions of others and turn them around so they actually work for our good.

This is a classic example of what Romans 8:28 tells us: _"We know that God causes all things to work together for good to those who love God, to those who are called according to His purpose."_

Because God is sovereign, He is able to accomplish His purpose through whatever life throws at us, and He does. He "causes _all_ things" to work toward His ultimate purpose. What an incredible principle!

> **"... you meant evil against me, but God meant it for good in order to bring about this present result, to preserve many people alive."**
> **—Joseph**
> **Genesis 50:20**

So how do I respond to the difficult circumstances that come my way? Do I just passively assume they are God's will and grit my teeth and bear them? We must recognize God's sovereignty, but we also are to actively address the things that face us.

A good evidence of this balance is seen in the experience of Paul's "thorn in the flesh." (2 Corinthians 12:7–10). In a sense, Paul's thorn in the flesh was a closed door, since God refused to remove it. What can we learn here about closed doors?

_____

_____

_____

_____

_____

> **"And we know that God causes all things to work together for good to those who love God, to those who are called according to His purpose."**
>
> **Romans 8:28**

How did Paul handle his "thorn in the flesh"? First, we know that this "thorn" was a messenger of Satan, but that hardly implies that it wasn't part of God's will. Satan often is used by God to accomplish His purposes (e.g. Job's trials, Christ's crucifixion, etc.). Paul trusted God's sovereignty, but he also actively sought the Lord's will in the situation. Three times he asked the Lord to take it away. When he finally discerned that this thorn was God's will, he had peace (Philippians 4:6–7) and became content.

So when we encounter divinely-designed circumstances, we are to actively seek the Lord about them, and when the signposts start lining up, we will discern His will.

❖　　❖　　❖　　❖　　❖　　❖　　❖　　❖　　❖

After receiving the crushing blow of my job rejection, I first responded by getting angry and bitter toward the committee. After all, was drawing names out of a hat any way to make important decisions? As I sought the Lord, however, and spent time in the Word, God reminded me that He is sovereign. I could make myself miserable focusing on the secondary causes, or I could trust God's sovereignty and know He can use anything and anyone to lead us. Proverbs 16:33 became a great comfort: *The lot is cast into the lap, but its every decision is from the LORD."*

Now, I'm not advising you to cast lots in making your decisions. Scripture presents many better and more mature ways to do that, but when life casts lots for you, trust that your sovereign Lord is able to direct the decision for your best. To me, God's sovereignty is one of His most attractive attributes. When it is coupled with His love and grace, it provides tremendous reassurance to the believer.

Why did God detour me from such a promising situation of working with my good friend and mentor? Because He is sovereign. He can see the things I can't see, and He knows what I need more than I do. We don't always get the chance to see clearly why God detours us (see 1 Corinthians 13:12), but in this case I did. Within a couple of months, God clarified this detour in leading me to join the staff of Campus Crusade for Christ.

Not only did God's detour protect me from suffering the consequences of a wrong choice, but it also provided for me in so many ways. What God detoured me to was a ministry that challenged me and stretched me in immeasurable ways. In my first two years on staff at the University of Virginia I was able to help plant a ministry at James Madison University that continues and thrives to this day. Most of the young men through which I invested my life while on staff are now either in full-time Christian ministry or have a significant impact as laymen.

Later, as director of Campus Crusade's ministry at the University of Tennessee, I was responsible for a ministry team of twelve full-time workers, an opportunity few pastors ever have. I was able, through our campus ministry, to be used in far broader ways than the church position would have provided, and that breadth of experience has been invaluable. Years later, when God moved me back onto the path of church ministry, I realized those experiences had done much to prepare me. God's detour protected me, and it provided for me, as only His will can.

FOR ME TO HEAR GOD

God is in charge! Because He is all-powerful, ever-present, and all-knowing, He is able to engineer the circumstances of our lives and use them to direct us toward His will. While the **DETOUR** signpost may be more prone to subjective interpretation than, say, the Scriptures, it is still one of the ways God speaks His will to us. We need to learn to hear what He says through our circumstances. Otherwise, we will become embittered slaves to the detours of life. But when we realize that God is willing and able to open or close any door to help us realize our calling and purpose in life, then the detours become friends instead of foes. Years ago, the president of the Billy Graham Evangelistic Association wrote a book entitled, *Turtle on a Fencepost*. The creative title came from an incident in the author's childhood. Walking down the road one day he saw a turtle sitting atop a fencepost, and immediately he knew that the turtle didn't get there by itself. He used that experience as an analogy for his life. He recognized that where he was in life was not the result simply of the things he had done, but rather, the things God had done. There is great freedom when we begin to recognize that God opens the doors that need to be opened to get us where He wants us to be. As we have seen in this lesson, a closed door isn't always a "no" from God, nor is an open door an automatic "yes." But we need to ask God what He is saying through our circumstances, for He does speak through open and closed doors.

 Ask yourself the following questions, and write the answers you believe will help you the most. Be honest!

1. What "open doors" or God-given barriers are there to consider in my situation?

_____

_____

_____

_____

> *A closed door isn't always a "no" from God, nor is an open door an automatic "yes." Yet we need to ask God what He is saying through our circumstances.*

2. For which trials or difficult circumstances do I need to seek guidance from the Lord?

_____

_____

_____

_____

_____

_____

_____

3. What is God saying to me through these circumstances?

_____

_____

_____

_____

_____

_____

_____

(You may need to come back to these as you work through other signposts in this book.)

Perhaps as you look back over your past, there are places where you stumbled over the circumstances life brought. As we saw in Day Four, providential circumstances made many choices for Joseph that he never would have chosen for himself. But in the end, Joseph trusted God's management of those circumstances, and saw them as evidence of His will. Situation after situation he found life sending him where he did not want to go. His jealous brothers sold him as a slave. The vindictive wife of his master had him thrown in prison on false charges. The man whom Joseph helped in prison forgot about him once he was set free. If most of us were faced with similar circumstances, we would be bitter and angry. But those who are embittered with life simply do not understand or trust God's sovereignty. In his two significant responses when questioned by his brothers about what had happened to him, Joseph teaches us the right way to trust God with the providential circumstances in our lives. Three times in Genesis 45, when his brothers are grieving, he basically says to them, "You didn't do this; God did this." In Genesis 50, he gives further clarity. He responds, "**You meant** *evil against me, but* **God meant** *it for good in order to bring about this present result, to preserve many people alive."*

APPLY Are there any situations from your past that make you bitter toward someone or some event?

_____

_____

_____

_____

Providential circumstances made many choices for Joseph that he never would have chosen for himself. But in the end, Joseph trusted God's management of those circumstances, and saw them as evidence of His will.

Write down the things from your past that you would change if it were possible.

_____

_____

_____

_____

_____

_____

Write down the things from your present that fall into the same category.

_____

_____

_____

_____

Now go through the lists and close out this lesson with a written prayer. To each item on the list, say to the Lord, "What they meant for evil, You meant for good." You may not yet be at the place Joseph described of being able to see the *present result,* but you can trust the Lord that He is working for a **good** result. One of the benefits of writing your prayer, as opposed to merely saying it, is that we tend to reflect more on written prayers, resulting in a more honest expression. Express your heart to Him in a written prayer.

_____

_____

_____

_____

_____

_____

_____

_____

_____

You may not be at the place Joseph described of being able to see the "present result," but you can trust the Lord that He is working for a good result!

Notes

THE REST AREA SIGN:
Peace

" I just have a peace about it, Eddie, Bob related. "I feel like this is the right thing to do." I had some questions about his wanting to back out of his commitment to go to the mission field, but this comment effectively shut my mouth. What else could I say? I strongly believe that every Christian is able to hear from God. We don't need an intermediary to tell us what God's will is, and yet I felt concern about Bob's decision.

I had known Bob for several years, and we were good friends. No one was more excited than I was when he told me he sensed God calling him to serve overseas. We had attended a Christian conference together, and at the end, Bob had surrendered every area of his life to Christ's control, including his plans for the future. It wasn't a great emotional experience. Rather, it was the culmination of all he was learning from the Word and of finally grasping that the most important things in life are the things that will last for eternity.

In the weeks and months that followed, God began to point Bob toward missions. He saw the eternal importance of fulfilling the great commission as he studied the Scriptures. He sensed God tugging at his heart as he prayed. Others advised that his success in his

"I just have a peace about it. . . ."

—"Bob"

personal ministry on campus showed that God could use him. Everything seemed to be pointing toward full-time Christian work. Even his parents, who he thought would be against the idea, surprised him with their support. He had applied with a mission agency and had been accepted to fill a post in Kenya. After graduation, Bob would go through six months of training, and after he raised his financial support, he would report to language school. Everything seemed to be falling into place.

Now some six months later, as graduation neared, Bob wasn't so sure. He had begun having doubts. His initial excitement had given way to many fears. "How will I ever find a wife in Kenya? I've never raised money before. . . I'm not sure I like the idea of asking people I don't know to give money. . . For that matter, I'm not too excited about asking my friends either."

In the stress and busyness of finals and graduation, Bob hadn't had much time to pray about his situation. In fact, he hadn't had much time to pray at all. His quiet times had been reduced to a quick couple of verses as he left for class. When he thought about going into ministry, he felt nervous and anxious, not excited. *Maybe that really isn't God's will,* he thought. *Maybe I just talked myself into it before.*

Bob was already wavering on the fence when the call came from his engineering professor telling Bob that he was recommending him for a tremendous government job. The more Bob thought about it, the more he believed, *Maybe this is what God wants me to do.* After all, the salary was exceptional. He would be able to give a lot of money to missions. He could stay in town, too. He'd have his friends to hang out with, and he could begin helping out with the youth group at his church. When the word came that he had gotten the job, Bob was ecstatic. He felt this job offer was the confirmation. "I just really have a peace about it, Eddie," he exclaimed as he related his decision. Had Bob found God's will, or had he strayed from it?

The next signpost to consider on our road to God's will is the **REST AREA** sign. One of the biblical synonyms of God's peace is what Hebrews 4 refers to as "rest." The **REST AREA** signpost is one of the most important we will talk about, partly because it is one of the most misunderstood and, therefore, one of the most misapplied. Because the concept of God's peace is linked to favorable emotions in most people's minds, it is often viewed as a feeling instead of a spiritual state of rest. Thus viewed, it becomes a subjective discipline instead of an objective criteria for discerning God's leading. This week's study will focus on seeing rest and peace as God does.

> *"There remains therefore a Sabbath rest for the people of God."*
>
> **Hebrews 4:9**

WHAT GOD'S PEACE IS NOT

Before we try to nail down what God's peace is, it will be extremely helpful to establish some parameters of what it is not. Having made these eliminations, it will be easier to hone in on exactly what God's peace is.

📖 John 14:27 identifies two types of peace. One is that which Jesus gives. What other type of peace does this verse allude to?

_____

_____

_____

From what you have observed, what role do circumstances play in the peace that the world gives?

_____

_____

_____

Since the peace that Christ gives is unlike what the world gives, how do you think it differs?

_____

_____

_____

The first and most essential distinction I've seen is that **God's peace is not circumstantial.** When Jesus spoke of His peace he said, *"Not as the world gives, do I give to you"* (John 14:27). The peace of the world is dictated only and always by circumstances. That is the only resource they have to find peace. But the peace of Christ is different than that.

📖 Look at Galatians 5:22–23. What is the source of God's peace?

_____

_____

_____

_____

_____

Scripture teaches us that God's peace is produced by the Holy Spirit, not by our circumstances (Galatians 5:22–23). This is borne out by the experience of saints throughout the ages. The peace of God, not circumstances, gave Stephen the confidence to preach truth as men took up stones to kill him. The peace of God, not circumstances, enabled Martin Luther to stand firm before the papal authority at the Diet of Worms. Most certainly, God's peace is not based on favorable circumstances.

I saw this principle some time back when my wife and I were flying home from the Southern Baptist Convention in New Orleans. We had just flown over Montgomery on our way to Atlanta when suddenly the plane banked sharply to the right and began dropping. Nothing was said over the loud-speakers but everyone knew something was seriously wrong. Stewardesses were falling all over the place as they tried frantically to secure everything that was loose. Our ears ached and our stomachs floated from the rapid, cork-screw-like drop in altitude. Babies were screaming and some adults wept openly while still others prayed out loud. My wife's knuckles were white as she gripped my hand.

God's peace is not circumstantial.

In less than five minutes we dropped from an altitude of 30,000 feet and approached a small airport. As we prepared to land we saw the fire engines, police cars and National Guard on the ground awaiting us. Once we landed we discovered that a bomb threat had been called in on our flight, and once we all had run safely to a nearby hangar, a cheer went up in unison. As our plane had descended, nothing in our circumstances dictated peace, yet my heart was flooded with it. I felt no anxiety, no fear. Whatever awaited us, my heart was at peace. The world does not give that peace.

The second observation I see is that **God's peace is not always logical.** It doesn't always mean that God's peace is illogical, but that it goes beyond mere human logic. Man's logic fails to factor in the power and sovereignty of God, something even believers don't fully understand or comprehend and unbelievers can't decipher at all.

Some time ago, my wife and I began having discipline problems with our oldest boy Blake, then four-and-a-half years old. It seemed that whatever we said, he did the opposite. We would give him instructions, and he would look right at us and disobey. It was as if our words didn't even register. These discipline problems had appeared so suddenly and were so uncharacteristic that my wife and I were left scratching our heads. What appeared suddenly in our son's behavior, however, soon spread to his health. Within a matter of a few days he went from an active, energetic four-year-old to total lethargy. He began to lose his motor skills and control of his bladder. He couldn't speak in any way but in a slow whisper. Our family physician immediately referred us to a neurosurgeon and we were prepared for the worst—a possible brain tumor.

As if our sons' health weren't enough to trust God with, we suffered added financial burdens as well. On the way to the doctor, the engine of our car blew out. We had been saving for some time to buy a house and a week before had put a $1000 deposit on one. With the car repairs and medical bills, our down-payment savings were gone quickly, and we had to face forfeiting our deposit and not buying a house. In circumstances like these you learn to live just in the present. You take each day as it comes; you face each problem as it comes. The present is enough for which to trust God without piling the future on as well.

As we endeavored to live in the present, we found ourselves holding our son's hands and praying as his lethargic and limp body was motored into the brain scan machine. As we prayed for our son, we acknowledged that he belonged to God, and we thanked God for giving him to us as long as He did. As we relinquished him to God, our hearts were flooded with a delicious sense of peace. We didn't know what the outcome would be, but we knew it lay in the hands of One we could trust. This was not logical peace from a human perspective, it wasn't man's peace—it was God's, and He doesn't give as the world gives.

One of the reasons God's peace doesn't always make sense at first is because God sees things that we don't. He already knew what we would later find out—that our son's problem was not a tumor, but viral encephalitis, a rare problem of a virus taking a wrong turn in the body and ending up in the nervous system. It results in inflammation and swelling of the brain, and God knew that although it sometimes results in permanent brain damage, in this case the recovery would be 100 percent! God also knew that although we didn't have the money to put down on our house, He would soon pro-

> "Peace I leave with you; My peace I give to you; not as the world gives, do I give to you. Let not your heart be troubled, nor let it be fearful."
>
> John 14:27

vide it through a surprise gift of $5,000. God's peace is beyond mere human logic because it comes from His vantage point, not ours.

What God's Peace Is

Well, we've seen what God's peace is not. It is not based on circumstances, and it is not always logical (humanly speaking). These are significant and fundamental observations. It is important that we draw Jesus' distinctions in our expectations of peace, or we will look for the same kind of peace that the world gives or seeks. But having shown some of these distinctions by defining what God's peace is not, now let's define what it is.

📖 Look at John 14:27 again. With what emotions does this verse contrast God's peace?

_____

_____

_____

_____

The best single description of God's peace is found in John 14:27, a verse I alluded to earlier. In it Jesus says: *"Peace I leave with you; My peace I give to you; not as the world gives, do I give to you. Let not your heart be troubled, nor let it be fearful."*

This verse relates an important distinction that demands notice: God's peace must be differentiated from the peace of the world. The world can give peace, but it is based on our circumstances and experienced in our feelings. God's peace is based on our being in the center of His will, and it is experienced not in our feelings, but in our spirit.

What is the message from Jesus in his statement, *"Let not your heart be troubled, nor let it be fearful"*?

_____

_____

_____

_____

The fact that Jesus admonishes us to not allow our hearts to be troubled or fearful is an acknowledgement that there is a choice involved. The world determines how to feel by what happens to them. The Christian, however, determines how to feel by his relationship with God. We are not to give in to the temptation to be troubled or fearful when circumstances do not go the way we desire.

In a nutshell, **God's peace is the absence of a troubled heart.** Like a diamond displayed on black velvet, it is most clearly seen when contrasted to difficult circumstances.

> *God's peace must be differentiated from the peace of the world. . . God's peace is based on our being in the center of His will, and it is experienced not in our feelings, but in our spirit.*

In John 16:32 we see some circumstances that would tend to lead one toward fear and anxiety. Identify in verse 33 the contrasting response that peace produces toward the world's tribulation.

_____

_____

_____

_____

There is nothing circumstantial in what the disciples were going to experience that would dictate an emotion-based peace. The disciples would be scattered. Jesus would be arrested, tried in a mock trial, and then crucified. Yet in the midst of this, Jesus promised His disciples God's peace. They would have internal victory while walking through external defeat. This is the promise and hope of Jesus overcoming the world.

Look at Philippians 4:6–7. What is the emotion that drives one to prayer, and how does the peace spoken of in verse 7 address that?

_____

_____

_____

_____

_____

This passage implies that it is often our own anxiety that moves us to prayer. This is how the Christian combats worry. We bring our requests and desires to an all-powerful God who can change whatever He wants. We may not always get what we request, but we will always have His peace that it is in His hands, not ours.

"But how does this kind of peace guide me toward God's will?" one would logically ask. It is important to recognize that peace or rest is **a spiritual state, a position of everything being right in my relationship with God.** If I am not obeying His leadings and His commands, my spirit will not know peace. If I am, then peace performs a confirming work in my heart. It is, however, subjective and prone to misinterpretation. My experience moves me to conclude that what I believe to be God's guiding peace is most dependable and most to be trusted when it goes against my circumstances. Everywhere peace is presented in Scripture, it is juxtaposed with anxiety. When I am peaceful about something that normally would make me anxious—this kind of peace comes only from God!

> *Everywhere peace is presented in Scripture, it is juxtaposed with anxiety. When I am peaceful about something I ought to be anxious about, that is God, not flesh.*

REST AREA

Day Three

PEACE

WHERE GOD'S PEACE ORIGINATES

Let's look back at Bob's decision in the introduction of this lesson. Was he experiencing God's peace or the world's? One of the things that concerned me was that his sense of peace contradicted how God had already led him up to that point. As we have already established, no one signpost stands alone, especially not one open to subjective interpretation like the **REST AREA** sign. As I listened to Bob and looked at his circumstances, I had to ask, "Does the peace you are experiencing come from God or from your circumstances?" That is not a question I as an outsider could answer. Only God and Bob could work it out. In my own decisions, distinguishing between God's peace and the world's has proven very helpful.

How do we get **God's peace** in our decisions? Scripture gives three specific instructions about how to obtain God's peace that have been an aid to me in my decision-making.

📖 Look at Galatians 5:22–23. If peace is a "fruit" of the Spirit, what do I need to do to access this peace?

_____

_____

_____

_____

Peace is identified in Galatians 5:22–23 as part of the "fruit of the Spirit": *"The fruit of the Spirit is love, joy,* **peace.***"* Peace is the fruit of **yielding to the Holy Spirit's control in my life.** If I am to have God's peace guarding my heart in any decision, He must be in control. If He is not, the only peace I can know is the peace of the world which is bound by circumstances.

📖 Read Isaiah 26:3. What does it teach about where God's peace originates?

_____

_____

_____

_____

Another essential to having God's peace is **keeping my eyes on Him**. Isaiah 26:3 states, *"Thou wilt keep him in perfect peace, whose mind is stayed on thee: because he trusteth in Thee"* (KJV). If we don't have peace in our decision, it could mean we have our eyes on circumstances instead of on the Lord. When Bob was seeking the Lord about his career, he had a peace about going into the ministry; but when he looked to his circumstances he no longer had peace. From where I sat, it appeared that his lack of peace about raising support wasn't from God but from his circumstances. God's peace comes from keeping our eyes on Him and trusting in Him.

The third essential to obtaining God's peace is **prayer.** We talked about this in a previous chapter, but let's review it here. Philippians 4:6–7 tells us that instead of being anxious, we are to pray, and the result will be that *"the peace of God, which surpasses all comprehension, shall guard your hearts and your minds in Christ Jesus."* Anxiety may be an indication that something is not God's will, but more often in my life it is a result of not adequately praying about a matter and putting it into God's hands, or a result of taking it back from a position of being surrendered to God. This anxiety is not God's leading but the world's worry. To which type of anxiety (God's or the world's) would you attribute Bob's concern about going into missions?

_____

_____

Did You Know?
THE FRUIT OF THE SPIRIT

When the Bible makes lists, often the most important item is mentioned first and the other items are expansions of the initial point. When Galatians refers to the *"fruit of the Spirit,"* it makes such a list. Notice it does not speak of the "fruits" of the Spirit. Many scholars believe the fruit of the Spirit is love, and the other items in the list are manifestations of love. In light of this week's lesson, this gives added meaning to the statement, *"There is no fear in love, but perfect love casts out fear"* (1 John 4:18).

📖 Look at the verses below and write what you learn about where God's peace originates.

Psalm 119:165

_____

_____

_____

Romans 8:6

_____

_____

_____

In Psalms 119:165 we glean an important component of being able to walk in God's peace: God's Word. What a powerful promise it is that those who _"love Thy law"_ (those who value and study His Word) have great peace and _"nothing causes them to stumble"_! The implication is that being in the Scriptures helps us avoid allowing our circumstances to rob us of God's peace. Romans 8:6 adds that a mind "set" on the Spirit is life and peace. So God's peace comes from continual study of His Word and a mind set on God's Spirit.

"Now when I came to Troas for the gospel of Christ and when a door was opened for me in the Lord, I had no rest for my spirit, not finding Titus my brother; but taking my leave of them, I went on to Macedonia."

2 Corinthians 2:12–13

What God's Peace Does

A s I related in the chapter on prayer (Signpost Two, Day Three) God's peace has a purpose. Philippians 4:7 tells us that when we have adequately prayed and surrendered an issue or a decision to God, His peace will guard our hearts and minds. The Greek word translated "guard" is a military term and refers to building a garrison to protect something. That is what God's peace does in the decision-making process. The power of God's peace protects my heart from fainting, from weakening, and it also protects my mind (literally, my thoughts), guarding them from anxiety.

📖 Read 2 Corinthians 2:12–13.

What does this passage teach about how God's peace or "rest" guided Paul?

_____

_____

_____

How did Paul's circumstances look, and what would he normally have done if it weren't for a lack of peace?

_____

_____

_____

Not only does God's peace guard me, but it also guides me. In 2 Corinthians 2:12–13 we see that Paul had all the right circumstances to minister in Troas, but God led him otherwise: *"Now when I came to Troas for the gospel of Christ and when a door was opened for me in the Lord, I had no rest for my spirit, not finding Titus my brother; but taking my leave of them, I went on to Macedonia."*

Paul had an open door, but he did not have God's peace. He had the right circumstances in which to minister, and the world's peace would have led him to stay. But God's peace combined with God's anxiety indicated otherwise. God's peace will guide us if we understand how to distinguish it from the world's circumstantial peace.

For Me to Hear God

As with every signpost, this one affords opportunities for misapplication. As I alluded to earlier, if we don't have peace about something, it may be that God is not leading us in that direction. However, in my experience with counseling others about God's will, I see a more prevalent reason for lack of peace in the decision-making process: lack of trust in God. Isaiah 26:3 tells us: *"Thou wilt keep him in perfect peace, whose mind is stayed on thee:* **because he trusteth in thee**" (KJV, emphasis mine). Hebrews 4:2 tells us that some do not experience God's positional rest because of unbelief. This verse refers directly to unbelievers, but later the passage (verse 11) applies the principle to believers. To experience God's rest, a synonym for peace, we must trust Him.

APPLY — As you consider your own decision-making, is there any evidence that a lack of peace is resulting from a faltering trust in God?

_____

_____

_____

Since peace is a fruit of the Spirit, you will not have peace apart from being Spirit-filled.

Have you given any recent decision over to God? If you answer yes, have you recently taken that decision-making back from Him?

_____

_____

_____

_____

_____

_____

Are you yielding your heart to His Spirit's control?

_____

_____

Another common danger in understanding God's peace is that it is so easy to misinterpret a lack of stress or problems as peace. As we saw before, peace that is truly from God is not dictated by circumstances. It is not external. It is internal and often in stark contrast to outside circumstances.

If peace is a result of keeping my eyes on the Lord, as Isaiah 26:3 teaches, then what does this say in your situation about why you might not have peace, even if you are following the Lord's will?

_____

_____

_____

As we look back at Bob's decision, we must ask ourselves, "Was he being guided by God's peace or by good circumstances?" God can and does use circumstances to direct us, so when circumstances are good, we cannot automatically conclude that we are in God's will. On the other hand, "bad circumstances" do not necessarily imply that we are apart from God's will.

In Bob's case, although circumstances pointed toward the good job, many other things had already pointed in another direction. The real enemy of God's best isn't usually something bad but something apparently good that is not of God's will.

Applying the Principles

APPLY Where are you in your search for God's will? Can you identify with Bob and his confusion over his circumstances? Ask yourself the questions below as you evaluate where you are, and apply this principle of peace as you seek to determine God's will.

1. Do I have a continued inner peace as I pray and consider the other signposts?

_____

_____

_____

_____

_____

_____

2. Do I have a sense of rest, allowing God to do the work, or do I sense the anxiety of my trying to make things work out?

_____

_____

_____

_____

_____

_____

_____

"The steadfast of mind Thou wilt keep in perfect peace, Because he trusts in Thee."

Isaiah 26:3

3. What evidence is there that my "peace," or lack of it, is merely circumstantial?

_____

_____

_____

_____

_____

_____

Why not take a moment to make sure your eyes are on the Lord and not on your circumstances, and reaffirm your trust in Him? As a future encouragement, write your prayer in the space below:

_____

_____

_____

_____

_____

_____

_____

_____

_____

_____

_____

Notes

THE "NO RIGHT TURN" SIGN:
The Holy Spirit

"What should I pray, Lord?" Susan silently implored. She had been trying for some time to pray for her sister, Darla, but just didn't know what to pray. Darla had been arrested at the Los Angeles airport with a suitcase full of cocaine and money.

Susan and her sister had grown up close. Being the only children of a broken marriage, they looked out for each other. Early in life, Susan started into drugs when she found out her sister did them. However, when Susan became a Christian as a freshman in college, the drug habits became a thing of the past. They continued for her sister, Darla, unfortunately.

The lawyer had told the family that since this was her second offense, they should be prepared for a fifteen-to-thirty-year sentence. Susan's heart was heavy and burdened, but the harder she tried to pray the harder the words came. She didn't want her only sister to go to prison, but as Susan prayed that she wouldn't, she knew in her heart it was not right to make such a request. Darla's first drug conviction resulted in three years probation, and this second conviction proved she had learned nothing from the first time. If she got off free this time, would Darla keep going the same direction? That really wasn't even a question

"And your ears will hear a word behind you, 'This is the way, walk in it,' whenever you turn to the right or to the left."

Isaiah 30:21

to be asked, though, because the whole family knew she wasn't going to get off free. But how should Susan pray?

There is no simple way to explain what happened next, but as clearly as if it were spoken out loud, Susan was impressed by a voice that spoke to her heart. The thought was planted in her mind: *Pray for a sentence of only five years.*

Now, before you start thinking "twilight zone" or that such ideas belong in the "looney bin," let me assure you this is not a regular occurrence in Susan's spiritual life. It certainly isn't in mine. Usually when God speaks to me, He does so through His saints or through the Scriptures. But there have been those times when I sensed God was speaking directly to me. This was such a time for Susan. On this occasion, God, by the Holy Spirit, spoke to her in her heart. If you have never experienced God speaking to you like this, I'm not sure I can help you understand what it means, but God spoke, and Susan knew that it was God speaking.

When there is a certainty that God has spoken, there is a confidence to act in faith. During the next few weeks, Susan asked every believer she knew to join her in praying that her sister would get only a five–year sentence. She shared this request with her church. She shared it with the Bible study group she was a part of. She shared it with her roommates. She shared it with the Christian group on campus in which she was involved. She asked every Christian she came in contact with to join her in trusting God for this very specific request. As the trial neared, her confidence grew, because she knew the petition she was placing before God did not originate with herself.

Finally the verdict came. On each of the three counts Susan's sister was to receive a ten–year sentence, but they were to run concurrently, the first five years in jail, the second five on probation. God took the most roundabout way possible to give her sister a five–year prison sentence. In the process, He greatly encouraged Susan's faith and that of those around her, especially her family. Those days of her sister's incarceration were hard on the family, and of course especially on Susan's sister, but God used them to do a real work of reconciliation both in Darla's relationship with God and in her relationship with the family. God does sometimes speak His will by that "still, small voice" of the Spirit (see 1 Kings 19:12 KJV).

> *Usually when God speaks, He does so through His saints or through the Scriptures. But there are times when God speaks directly to us in our hearts.*

"NO RIGHT TURN" SIGN

Day One

THE HOLY SPIRIT

THE LEADING OF THE HOLY SPIRIT

The next signpost on the way to God's will is the **NO RIGHT TURN** sign.

📖 In Isaiah 30:21 we are given a glimpse of one of the ways God speaks His will.

What is the context of this verse?

_____

_____

_____

_____

What does this verse have to say about this means of communication from the Lord?

_____

_____

_____

What practical things are implied here?

_____

_____

_____

Isaiah 30:21 tells us, *"And your ears will hear a word behind you, 'This is the way, walk in it' whenever you turn to the right or to the left."* I have experienced that voice, not often, but at crucial junctures in my spiritual walk. As we consider ways God speaks His will, do not underestimate the possibility that He may speak it by His Spirit who indwells us. I link this spiritual voice with the **NO RIGHT TURN** sign because most often we hear the voice of the Spirit, not when we are on the path of God's will, but when we turn from it *"to the right or to the left"* as Isaiah points out.

To better understand the leading of the Holy Spirit, it will be helpful if we understand more about the Holy Spirit Himself and consider how He ministers.

As a child, I found the concept of the Holy Spirit difficult to understand. When we sang those final words of the Doxology at church, "Praise Father, Son, and Holy Ghost," my juvenile mind conjured up an image of Casper the Friendly Ghost with a halo. The Scriptures make it clear, however, that the Holy Spirit is a person, not an amorphous, impersonal force akin to something from Star Wars. He is as much God as Jesus or the Father, yet He is often the most misunderstood person of the Trinity.

📖 Look at Romans 8:14 and write what you learn of one of the Spirit's roles in the life of the believer.

_____

_____

_____

_____

_____

_____

_____

The Word of God clarifies several ways the Holy Spirit works in our lives. Perhaps the most relevant passage on the subject of God's will is Romans 8:14: *"All who are being* **led by the Spirit of God** *. . . are sons of God."* If I am a child of God, I will experience the Holy Spirit's leading. This verse is not open to debate. It doesn't mean that I always follow the Spirit's leading, but if I never experience the Spirit's leading, then I am not a Christian! Christians may debate how the Holy Spirit will lead, but hopefully this passage makes it clear to all sides that the Holy Spirit does play a role in leading the believer.

"My sheep hear My voice, and I know them, and they follow Me."

John 10:27

"NO RIGHT TURN" SIGN

Day Two

THE HOLY SPIRIT

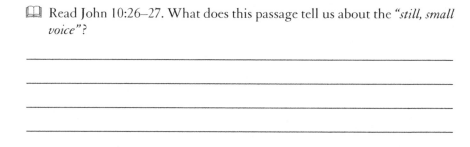

📖 Read John 10:26–27. What does this passage tell us about the *"still, small voice"*?

_____

_____

_____

_____

Jesus told the unbelieving Jews, *"You do not believe, because you are not of My sheep. My sheep hear My voice, and I know them, and they follow Me"* (John 10:26–27). The point is clear: if Jesus is speaking to us, we will recognize the voice as His. We see this principle revealed time after time, as God has spoken to different people in Scripture.

How Does the Lord Speak?

How exactly do we hear His voice? As I related in Day One, one of the ways we hear God's voice is through listening to His Spirit who lives within us. That is what Susan experienced when she sought God's will in how to pray for her sister. Lest we think of this as a subjective, unbiblical experience, I think it is valuable to look at examples in Scripture.

📖 Look at Matthew 4:1.

What is the Spirit's action here?

_____

_____

_____

Practically speaking, how do you suppose this happened?

_____

_____

_____

Here in Matthew 4:1 we see this principle of the Spirit's leading modeled in the life of Jesus. Christ is "led" by the Spirit into the wilderness to be tempted by the devil. We are not told any specific details here on how this leading took place, but we can conclude from other passages that it was an inner impression, as there is no indication of any audible voice.

📖 Read Mark 2:8. Look at the story and determine how the Spirit communicated with Jesus in this incident.

_____

_____

_____

_____

📖 *Doctrine*
SPIRITUAL WARFARE

Jesus' temptation in the wilderness makes it clear that sometimes it is God's will for us to face spiritual battle. Jesus is *"led up by the Spirit"* into the wilderness to be tempted by the devil. Satan had hopes of defeating the Lord, but God had the intention of affirming Jesus through this encounter. While we are not to go looking for the devil, we cannot expect to fully avoid encountering his temptations.

When Jesus healed the paralytic and forgave his sins, the scribes were indignant. They could not accept that a mere man could forgive sins, and they were not willing to admit that Jesus might be more than just a mere man. They said nothing, but in their minds they thought, "Blasphemy!" Here in Mark 2:8 we see that Jesus was *aware in His spirit* of what they were thinking. Another way of translating this from the Greek is "aware <u>by</u> His Spirit."

John 16:7–9 tells us that the Holy Spirit leads by conviction in three specific areas: **sin, righteousness, and judgment.** The same Spirit who first convinced me of the truth of the gospel indwells me and lets me know when I stray from God's desire. He points me in the direction of righteousness. And when I stubbornly go my own way, He reminds me of judgment. Conviction is one way God speaks His will, and He does that speaking by the Holy Spirit who lives in us.

📖 Look at Acts 16:6–7. What do these verses indicate the Spirit did in Paul's ministry?

_____

_____

_____

_____

We looked at these verses in a previous lesson on detours, but here we see them in the light of <u>how</u> the Spirit detoured Paul. We see on the one side that Paul was *"forbidden by the Holy Spirit"* to speak the Word in Asia, and on the other side, that the *"Spirit of Jesus"* (another way of denoting the Holy Spirit) did not permit them to go into Bithynia. It is significant that the grammatical structure in the Greek indicates that Paul kept trying to go into Bithynia, and was not allowed. Though we are not told here how the Spirit communicated with Paul, we see clearly that He did.

Another incident of the Spirit's leading is found in Acts 8:25–40. It is the account of Philip's ministry with the Ethiopian eunuch on the Gaza road. Read the story and answer the questions below.

Philip is returning to Jerusalem from ministry in Samaria when he is redirected to go south from Jerusalem toward Gaza. Look at a Bible map and familiarize yourself with where these geographical references are located.

How is Philip redirected to the Gaza road (verse 26)?

_____

_____

_____

How is Philip directed to the chariot of the Ethiopian official (verse 29)?

_____

_____

_____

_____

Did You Know?

NAMES OF THE HOLY SPIRIT

Like God the Father, and God the Son, God the Spirit is known by many different names, each communicating something different of His character. Some notable names in Scripture are. . . .

- ❏ The Holy Spirit
- ❏ The Spirit of God
- ❏ The Helper
- ❏ The Spirit of Christ
- ❏ The Comforter
- ❏ The Spirit of Jesus

What was the result of this encounter?

_____

_____

_____

_____

_____

Word Study
HOLY SPIRIT

The Greek word for Holy Spirit (_Paráklētos_) means **1)** summoned, called to one's side, especially called to one's aid; **2)** one who pleads another's cause before a judge, a pleader, a counsel for defense, a legal assistant, an advocate; **3)** one who pleads another's cause with one, an intercessor of Christ in his exaltation at God's right hand, pleading with God the Father for the pardon of our sins; **4)** in the widest sense, a helper, a succorer, an aider, an assistant; used of the Holy Spirit destined to take the place of Christ with the apostles (after Christ's ascension to the Father), to lead them to a deeper knowledge of the gospel truth, and to give them divine strength needed to enable them to undergo trials and persecutions on behalf of the divine kingdom.

In this brief narrative from the book of Acts, we see a significant example of the Spirit's leading. Philip is returning from ministry in Samaria (the region to the north of Jerusalem) when an angel appears to him and tells him to go south to _"the road that descends from Jerusalem to Gaza"_ (a town near the Mediterranean coast, located southwest of Jerusalem). Once on the road, Philip encounters a chariot and is told by the Spirit to go up to the chariot. He finds a man there who is spiritually hungry and leads him to faith in Christ. While the story is noteworthy in itself, it also reveals an interesting truth about how the Spirit speaks to us.

To fully understand this incident, a Greek lesson is in order. When Luke tells us in Acts 8:26 that an angel of the Lord "spoke" to Philip, the Greek word translated "spoke" is _laleō_. It literally means "to break the silence" and has the idea of an audible noise. When Acts 8:29 tells us that the Spirit "said" to Philip to go up to the chariot, Luke uses a different Greek word for "said." It is the word _eípon,_ a strengthened form of the word _légō_, which means "to communicate a message." This word doesn't necessarily mean to communicate verbally. It places the emphasis, not on **how** the message is communicated, but on the fact **that** the message is communicated.

You may be saying, "It certainly is Greek to me!" What does all this technical vocabulary information have to do with how the Spirit speaks? First of all, we must understand that the Greek language, of which the New Testament was originally written, is a far more precise language than English. When biblical authors change from using one word to another, often there is a subtle but significant distinction being drawn. While studying this passage, I asked myself the question, "Why does Luke use _légo_ instead of _laléo_ when he describes the speaking of the Spirit?" What I found is that when you go through the whole New Testament, the word _laléo_ (verbal speech) is never used of the Holy Spirit speaking. In every case a form of _légō_ (communicated message) is used. To me this argues strongly that when the Spirit speaks to us, it is in fact that "still, small voice" in our hearts that saints down through the ages have described. I have never had God speak to me audibly (I'm a Baptist, and He knows I couldn't handle that), but I have heard the still, small voice of the Spirit speaking to my heart. That is one of the ways God leads us.

"NO RIGHT TURN" SIGN

Day Three

THE HOLY SPIRIT

THE TEACHING MINISTRY OF THE SPIRIT

Another ministry of the Holy Spirit is that He **teaches us and reminds us of God's truth.** When it comes to spiritual matters, we have an indwelling tutor to guide us through the learning process.

📖 Look up John 14:26 and write what you learn there about the ministry of the Holy Spirit and how He speaks to us.

What two functions does this passage identify that the Holy Spirit plays in our lives?

_____

_____

How do they differ from each other?

_____

_____

_____

_____

On Christ's last evening with the disciples before His death, He spent most of His time helping them understand the ministry of the coming Holy Spirit. The result is the richest and fullest teaching in all of Scripture on the person of the Holy Spirit (John 14—16). One of the points Christ makes in this powerful passage is that He, our "Helper" as Christ called Him, *"will teach you all things, and bring to your remembrance all that I said to you"* (John 14:26). It is through the work of the Holy Spirit that we understand the truths of God's Word. It is also through His ministry that pertinent Scriptures are called to mind when we need them. We see this ministry illustrated numerous times in the lives of the apostles.

📖 Read Ephesians 6:17. What is the role of the Spirit here in spiritual warfare?

_____

_____

_____

_____

This ministry of the Holy Spirit calling to mind Scripture at my time of need is what Paul refers to in Ephesians 6:17 when he speaks of the *"sword of the Spirit, which is the word of God."* The Greek word that is translated "word" here is not *logos*, the general term normally used. Instead Paul uses *rhema*, indicating "spoken words," Scriptures which God speaks to our heart by His Spirit as we need them. Often as we seek God's will about a choice we are to make or a path we want to pursue, He answers us by the Holy Spirit calling to our mind a verse that tells us what we need to know.

📖 Look up John 16:13–15 and write what you learn there about how the Holy Spirit ministers to us.

_____

_____

_____

_____

THE HOLY SPIRIT

"But when He, the Spirit of truth, comes, He will guide you into all the truth; for He will not speak on His own initiative, but whatever He hears, He will speak; and He will disclose to you what is to come. He shall glorify Me; for He shall take of Mine, and shall disclose it to you." (John 16:13–15)

In Christ's upper–room discourse, He also revealed another way the Holy Spirit ministers: by revealing and disclosing truth. John 16:13–15 teaches us that the Holy Spirit is able to *"guide you into all the truth. . . . He takes of Mine, and will disclose it to you."*

Of course, this revealing and disclosing ministry relates to the Bible and never contradicts the clear teaching of the Scriptures. Sometimes, however, as with Susan's need for wisdom in how to pray for her sister, the Holy Spirit discloses God's wisdom to our hearts in a specific way to guide us.

"NO RIGHT TURN" SIGN

Day Four

THE HOLY SPIRIT

SOME DANGERS WITH THIS SIGNPOST

As with each of the signposts directing us to God's will, this one is not without its dangers. Hearing the voice of the Spirit and recognizing His leading is contingent on several factors. First, although all believers can hear and recognize the voice of their Shepherd, in my own life that process becomes easier as I mature in my walk with Christ. Hearing and recognizing His voice implies a relationship. For my relationship with Christ to be effective, it must be developed.

📖 Read 1 Samuel 3:1–14.

What does Samuel think when he hears the voice calling (verses 5, 6, 8)?

_____

_____

_____

Who finally discerns that it is the Lord speaking (verse 8)?

_____

_____

What does this say about maturity helping us discern the Lord's voice?

_____

_____

_____

_____

We need to be careful when applying a story like this from the Old Testament. It is not exactly the same thing as the voice of the Spirit that we are studying this week, for here God speaks audibly. But there are some principles we can glean that relate to our study. The first and also the main principle is that Samuel was not spiritually mature, and it is the older prophet Eli who first recognizes that God is speaking to Samuel and helps him come to that conclusion. It is not a lesson that will have to be repeated, for Samuel becomes adept at recognizing the voice of God.

The second principle we learn from Samuel is that hearing and recognizing the voice of God requires keeping short accounts with Him about sin. If there is sin in my life, and I know it but have not dealt with it God's way, the only words I will hear from God will be convicting words regarding that sin. Any other voice I hear will not be God's, but the voice of the world, my flesh, or the devil. This unholy trio speaks louder when my walk with Christ is dirtied by sin, and any one of them can be quite deceiving. Scripture teaches that Satan sometimes disguises himself as an angel of light, and I must remember that. The surest safeguard to rightly applying this signpost of the Spirit is to make sure my walk with God is healthy and unhindered by sin, and to ask God to confirm His leading with other signposts as well.

📖 Look at 1 Thessalonians 5:19–22.

What does this passage indicate about what might interrupt the Spirit's ministry in our lives?

_____

_____

_____

What picture does the phrase *"quench the Spirit"* paint?

_____

_____

_____

Based on this passage, how do you think we might quench God's Spirit?

_____

_____

_____

It is significant that the statement *"Do not quench the Spirit"* is linked with the admonition *"Do not despise prophetic utterances."* The idea of "quenching" the Spirit paints a picture of dousing a fire with water. Often the Spirit is pictured in Scripture as fire (as in the day of Pentecost—Acts 2). This suggests that we can douse the fires of the Spirit's leading in our lives when we fail to respond to the Spirit's prompting. Some call this "sins of omission"— failing to obey the Lord's leading, which is essentially omitted obedience. This idea is balanced with the warning to examine everything carefully. We are not to go off half-cocked spiritually, jumping at every whim and assuming it is the Spirit. But when we have a prompting, we must investigate it scripturally and not neglect it. When we see it confirmed by other indicators, we must act in faith. Failing to respond to the Spirit's prompting will dull our spiritual hearing.

📖 Read Ephesians 4:29–32.

What does this passage indicate about what might interrupt the Spirit's ministry in our lives?

_____

_____

_____

If I know there is sin in my life and am not dealing with it God's way, the only words I will hear from God will be convicting words relating to that sin. Any other voice I hear will not be God's, but the voice of the world, my flesh, or the devil.

What picture does the phrase *"grieve the Spirit"* paint?

_____

_____

_____

How do you think from this passage we might do that?

_____

_____

_____

Did You Know?

RESPONDING TO THE HOLY SPIRIT

There are four verses which mention specific ways we relate to the Spirit negatively. We can...

- ❑ Grieve the Spirit—Ephesians 4:30
- ❑ Quench the Spirit—I Thessalonians 5:19
- ❑ Resist the Spirit—Acts 7:51
- ❑ Insult the Spirit—Hebrews 10:29

Here we see a different side of interrupting the Spirit's work. We are admonished to not *"grieve the Spirit."* The picture painted is to wound, to hurt, to cause emotional pain. We cause grief to the Spirit when we violate the clear commands of the Lord. Some call these "sins of commission"—doing things we are commanded not to do, essentially **committing** acts that are wrong as opposed to **omitting** actions that are right. The context speaks of a number of specific prohibitions. Failing to stay within the Spirit's boundaries will dull our spiritual hearing.

📖 A good passage to keep in mind when seeking to follow the Lord is Psalm 32:8–9. What dangers does it reveal of missing the Lord's leading?

_____

_____

_____

_____

This passage reveals God's commitment to show us His will—and two dangers of missing His leading: *"I will instruct you and teach you in the way which you should go; I will counsel you with My eye upon you. Do not be as the horse or as the mule which have no understanding."*

Think of the analogies being used. A horse tends to run ahead, and the bit and bridle must be pulled to hold him in check. On the other hand, the mule tends to lag behind in stubbornness, and must be dragged and kicked.

Many Christians follow God the same way a horse or a mule does. Either they run ahead of God without waiting to hear from Him or they lay behind in stubbornness and won't step out in faith. Which is your tendency? Mine is running ahead of God, but I have learned the hard way that it is better to find His will the first time than to be taught it by consequences.

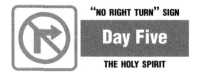

"NO RIGHT TURN" SIGN

Day Five

THE HOLY SPIRIT

FOR ME TO HEAR GOD

As you seek God's will, remember it is not like an Easter-egg hunt where He has done His best to hide it and you must try to find it. God wants you to know His will even more than you do, and He will show it to you if you let Him. But to hear that *"still, small voice,"* you must monitor your relationship with Him. Consider the following questions and record your answers here:

APPLY Do you sense God is motivating you toward or away from a particular course of action?

_____

_____

If so, what?

_____

_____

Are you behaving as a horse in this situation (running ahead of God)?

_____

_____

_____

If so, what do you need to do differently to take time to listen to Him?

_____

_____

Are you behaving as a mule in this situation (lagging behind because of your stubbornness or unbelief)?

_____

_____

_____

If so, what do you need to do differently to take the steps of faith He wants you to take?

_____

_____

_____

_____

Are you sure that you are filled with the Holy Spirit (Eph. 5:18) and that there is no unconfessed sin in your heart?

_____

_____

_____

> **God's will is not like an Easter-egg hunt where He has done His best to hide it and you must try to find it. God wants you to know His will even more than you do.**

To be sure we are filled with the Spirit, we must look at the barriers we studied in Day Four. We cannot become Christians without allowing Christ to take control of our lives. We surrender to Him, and He moves into our lives. While scripture passages like Hebrews 13:5 (_"I will never leave thee nor forsake thee"_ | KJV]) make it clear that He will always be **resident** in our lives, that doesn't mean He is **president**. We can again seize control of our lives through sins of commission or sins of omission. If we have taken charge of our lives, we will disconnect from our source of spiritual power. Bill Bright effectively expresses the solution when he relates the principle he calls "Spiritual Breathing." Simply put, when we take control of our lives through direct disobedience to the Word of God, or through neglected obedience to the leading of God, we must breathe spiritually. When we breathe physically, we exhale the impure air, and inhale the pure. The same process occurs in our spiritual lives during repentance. We exhale the impure through confession, and inhale the pure through yielding.

Why not practice this principle with anything that the Lord has convicted you in this lesson.

Exhale—confess any sins the Lord has brought to mind.
First John 1:9 promises, *"If we confess our sins, He is faithful and righteous to forgive us our sins and to cleanse us from all unrighteousness."* The word "confess" is in the present tense in the Greek meaning continual, repeated action. It refers not to the initial confession of sins at salvation, but the ongoing confession of maintaining fellowship with God.

Inhale—yield control of your life back to Christ.
Ephesians 5:18 instructs us, *"Do not get drunk with wine, for that is dissipation, but be filled with the Spirit."* It is a command, meaning it is a choice on which we must act.

It is the regular practice of spiritual breathing that keeps our ears spiritually sensitive to the promptings of the Holy Spirit.

Why not write out a prayer of yieldedness here to confirm your commitment?

_____

_____

_____

_____

_____

_____

_____

_____

_____

Notes

Notes

THE CARPOOL SIGN:
Stewardship

To be honest, Steve's comment caught me a little off guard. Someone had asked him how God led him to join the staff of Campus Crusade for Christ. I was still very young in the Lord and somewhat naive in this matter of how God communicated His will, and I must admit that at first I was a little disappointed with his response.

"There were many things to consider," he said, "but the major issue for me came down to stewardship."

I had expected something far more dramatic, like a vision at the end of an all-night prayer vigil. It seemed to me that God calling someone to the ministry ought to be a special, almost mystical experience. Stewardship certainly didn't fit my perception.

The group inquired further, and Steve explained the process he had gone through to determine God's will for his vocation. In college, he majored in business and planned to get his MBA after graduation. Through his involvement with Campus Crusade during his undergraduate years, he had introduced several classmates to Christ and had a discipleship group that God had blessed tremendously. In fact, all three of the young men he discipled in his last two years of college now had disciples of their own.

"...moreover, it is required of stewards that one be found trustworthy."

I Corinthians 4:2

During the summers, Steve had participated in mission projects, one in a resort area in California, and two overseas. He felt that the training and experience of those projects had made a profound impact on his walk with Christ and his personal ministry. He also attended numerous Campus Crusade conferences and further developed his evangelism and discipleship skills.

Toward the end of his junior year, Steve began thinking about full-time ministry. During the orientation for his missions project that summer, one of the leaders made a statement that startled him. The leader said, "I realize that many of you may feel inadequate to minister in some of the situations you will find yourselves. The truth is, though, that you already know more about the Bible and have more ministry experience than most of the pastors you will be working with in this part of Africa."

Steve had never considered himself a spiritual giant by any stretch of the imagination, yet he was surprised to learn that only about five percent of Christians have a personal ministry; less than two percent share their faith on a regular basis; and only one percent disciple others to do these things.

On his mission project, Steve worked with an African national named Idirishu. Everything in Idirishu's life was surrendered to the Lord and to the cause of reaching his countrymen for Christ, and he was a challenge to be around.

Steve asked him what motivated him to minister, and Idirishu answered, "I am wanting to be found a faithful steward. Everything I have, God has given to me, and one day I will answer to Him for how I used it. When I have money, I must spend it in ways that honor Him. The time I have must be managed like money. The truth God teaches me, I am a steward of, and I must share it with others."

"That last statement spoke to me the most," Steve told us. "I never really considered that what God had taught me was as much something to be a steward of as my time or money or abilities."

As Steve related, 2 Timothy 2:2 tells us that we are to entrust the truth God teaches us to *"faithful men, who will be able to teach others also."*

As he applied that principle to his own life, Steve realized that many people around him could be businessmen, but few knew how to have a ministry. "I looked at the biblical teaching and ministry training God had entrusted to me, and it didn't make sense to use it only in my spare time. The needs of the world are too great. Coming on staff seemed the best way to be a good steward of all God had built into my life."

That's when I began to realize that God reveals His will in many different ways.

> ## "The time I have must be managed like money. The truth God teaches me, I am a steward of, and I must share it with others."
> ### —Idirishu (an African Pastor)

CARPOOL SIGN

Day One

STEWARDSHIP

THE CALL TO STEWARDSHIP

The next signpost we encounter on our road to God's will is the **CARPOOL** sign. This sign pops up more and more frequently around major cities with gas prices continuing to rise and pollution remaining an ever-present problem. The **CARPOOL** sign reminds us to be good stewards of everything over which we have dominion, including our money and our planet. Godly stewardship, an important principle in the Scriptures, is one area through which God speaks His wisdom.

📖 Look at Matthew 25:14–30.

What is the main message of this parable?

_____

_____

How did the master reward those stewards who had proven themselves faithful?

_____

_____

_____

The book of Matthew contains what is known as the Olivet Discourse, a conversation Christ had with His disciples. In this discourse, He relates a series of parables, of which one of the most familiar is the Parable of the Talents. Three men are given talents (bars of gold or silver) to manage for their master. One receives five talents, one receives two, and one receives only one. The first two faithfully invested their talents, and when their master returned they had doubled the amounts. The third steward hid his talent and had nothing more when the master returned.

This parable contains an important message for us: We are stewards of all that is entrusted to us, and one day we will give an account. But there is another, less obvious message in this parable. It is found in what was done with the talent managed by the unfaithful steward—it was taken away and given to the faithful steward.

Do you ever wonder why some people seem to get many natural opportunities to share Christ while others have so few? From what I have observed in ministry, I believe that opportunities to minister are given by God in response to our proven faithfulness. Those who are faithful in the small opportunities to serve receive greater opportunities. Those who are not faithful lose what opportunities they originally had, and, subsequently, they lead insignificant lives. I'm not saying that all worthwhile service is flashy and noticed by others, or that all serve the same way, or that all see the same results. But I am saying that those who are good stewards of the opportunities to minister, using what God gives them, will lead eternally significant lives even if those souls are unnoticed here on earth.

📖 Look at Psalm 78:70–72 in light of the principles we have observed so far and record your observations.

_____

_____

_____

_____

_____

Did You Know?

WHAT IS A "TALENT"?

A talent was a weight composed of about 120 pounds. When used in the monetary sense, the talent might be either of silver or gold; and the value varied according to the standard. If an ounce of gold is now worth roughly $300, then a talent of gold would be worth $576,000 in today's dollars. A talent of silver (at $4 an ounce) would be worth nearly $7,700. In either case, five or ten talents would be a great amount of money for which to be accountable.

> **"And from everyone who has been given much shall much be required; and to whom they entrusted much, of him they will ask all the more."**
>
> **Luke 12:48**

This really is a powerful statement about God's choosing of David. We know that David was a man after God's own heart. Here we see that David had already proven his faithfulness as a shepherd, when God chose to give him a larger herd: Israel. David had risked his life to faithfully protect the flock under his charge. Scripture tells us he killed both a lion and a bear in the process. He would apply that same kind of heart in leading Israel. David was faithful in small things and was placed in charge of large ones.

📖 What does 1 Corinthians 4:2 have to say about what is required of a steward?

_____

_____

_____

It is not a requirement of a steward that one be perfect, but that he be found trustworthy or faithful. He must be dependable. It is a significant realization when we recognize that we really own nothing. We are merely stewards of the things God has entrusted to us, and this stewardship is only for a season.

📖 Read Luke 12:42–48. What is the main point that Jesus makes here (*Note verse 48)?

_____

_____

_____

The main point Jesus makes in Luke 12 is summed up in verse 48: "To whom much is given, much is required." The greater our blessing, the greater our accountability. We will one day answer to the Lord not just according to what we did, but according to what we did with what He gave us.

CARPOOL SIGN

Day Two

STEWARDSHIP

Stewardship and the Will of God

The Bible assures us that part of God's will for our lives is to be good stewards of all He entrusts to us. The question to ask ourselves is, *Will this decision I am making result in my being a good steward?* Perhaps I am considering a purchase. *Would that purchase demonstrate good stewardship of the money God entrusts to me?* Perhaps I am trying to decide on something involving a substantial time commitment. *Will this decision reflect good stewardship of my time?* As we can see from Steve's experience, understanding stewardship becomes an important resource in evaluating career choices.

📖 Look up the verses below and see what they have to say about God's ownership of us and all we possess.

Psalm 100:3

_____

_____

_____

Isaiah 64:8

_____

_____

_____

In Psalm 100 we see two powerful truths. First, it is God who has made us—we did not create ourselves! Not only is He our Creator, but it is He who has made us what we are. Second, we belong to Him. We are <u>HIS</u>. We are His people, and we live in His pasture (the earth He created). Isaiah 64 calls us the clay in the hands of Him, our potter. We are the work of His hands.

When we seek God's will, it has to begin with an acknowledgement that He has every right to expect and even demand our faithful stewardship of everything He chooses to entrust to us.

📖 Look up these verses and see what they have to say about God's ownership of us and all we possess.

1 Chronicles 29:11–16

_____

_____

_____

2 Corinthians 5:14–15

_____

_____

_____

We see here in 1 Chronicles that **everything** in the heavens and earth belongs to God. Even when we give to God, we are only giving back out of what He has given us. Not only does everything we have belong to God because He made us, but we are doubly His. As 2 Corinthians 5 points out, we have been bought by the blood of Christ. He didn't die for us so we could live selfish, greedy lives. He died for us so that we could live for Him as stewards of His blessings.

What a Steward Is a Steward of

If I am called to be a steward, and if one day I will give an account to God for my stewardship, then I need to know over what things I am to be a steward. The Scriptures spell out four precious commodities which must be managed prudently. Understanding these aids me greatly in knowing God's will for my life.

The first commodity over which each believer is to be a steward is **time**. The President of the United States has the same number of hours in his week as I do. A significant life is not a result of how much time I have, but of how I use that time.

"But who am I and who are my people that we should be able to offer as generously as this? For all things come from Thee, and from Thy hand we have given Thee."

1 Chronicles 29:14

CARPOOL SIGN
Day Three
STEWARDSHIP

CARPOOL LANE

📖 Read Ephesians 5:15–16.

What is the call of these verses?

_____

_____

What are the two possibilities mentioned?

_____

_____

What is the reason given for the challenge?

_____

_____

Ephesians 5:15–16 exhorts us, *"Therefore be careful how you walk, not as unwise men, but as wise, making the most of your time, because the days are evil."* We are called to be careful. There is in each day, and even each hour, the potential of being wise or of being unwise. The challenge to make the most of our time is given because the days are evil. In other words, if unplanned, time does not tend to move in directions of godliness.

Time is a perishable commodity: it is not eternal. Once used, it is gone forever, leaving in its place what I traded it for. A good evaluation question is, Was it worth it? Was my use of that time worth what I have to show for it? The key here is balance. For example, I can't use stewardship as an excuse for not sleeping or not spending time with my family. I must balance my priorities.

The next area of stewardship is my **talents.** Every person has certain God-given abilities, both natural and spiritual, that make him unique, and God desires that those abilities be used to the fullest. A year or so ago a young man asked my advice on what he should do when he graduated from college. He had some job prospects, but he was also a world-class distance runner and could make a living for a while doing that. As I helped him through the process of making the decision, I reminded him of this issue of stewardship. While stewardship alone didn't guarantee that it was God's will for him to continue running, it certainly was a major factor. Few of us can lay claim to being a world-class anything, much less a world-class athlete. I encouraged him to consider the tremendous platform for ministry which athletics brings and to ask God if that might be His will for now. His business degree could be picked up later, but his running couldn't.

📖 Look at 1 Peter 4:10–11.

What do these verses say is true of every believer?

_____

_____

What are we to do with our spiritual gifts?

_____

_____

Doctrine
SPIRITUAL GIFTS

The New Testament gives four different lists of spiritual gifts, and there is no indication that together they are exhaustive. They are. . .

☐ Romans 12:3–8

☐ I Corinthians 12:1–31

☐ Ephesians 4:11–12

☐ I Peter 4:10–11

Who is to benefit from them?

_____

_____

_____

Certainly natural abilities such as athletic prowess or artistic giftedness are resources to be managed, but not all of us have significant talents in these areas. Scripture teaches, however, that every believer does have spiritually-endowed abilities over which God calls Him to be a steward. The Bible refers to these as "spiritual gifts." In 1 Peter 4:10 we are told: _"As each one has received a special gift, employ it in serving one another, as good stewards of the manifold grace of God."_ The fact that every Christian has at least one gift guarantees that the gifts are important. The church will not be what it could or should be without the exercise of the spiritual gifts of its people. Each Christian is called to "employ" that gift not for his own benefit, but to the benefit of others.

Our spiritual gifts can be neglected (1 Timothy 4:14), or they can be developed (2 Timothy 1:6). To be good stewards we must exercise those gifts in such a way that they minister to others, not just ourselves (1 Peter 4:10), and they must glorify God, not us (1 Peter 4:11).

For Steve, both his abilities and his gift were important factors in his career choice, as they are for all of us. Almost every profession has certain required abilities or gifts that not everyone else has. Not all of us, even with the same effort, could play pro football. How are you gifted? What are your strengths and abilities? God will call you to account for how you use them.

The third area of stewardship, perhaps the most often mentioned aspect, is stewardship of our **treasures,** the financial resources we are given, or that we develop. Like time, money is also a perishable commodity; once used it is gone, leaving behind what it was traded for. It is not eternal, but, like time, it can be invested in things that are eternal.

📖 Look at the challenge in Luke 16:11–12. What does this passage parallel our use of money with?

_____

_____

_____

_____

Money, like time, can be wasted. Luke 16:11–12 related a somber warning: _"If therefore you have not been faithful in the use of unrighteous mammon, who will entrust the true riches to you? And if you have not been faithful in the use of that which is another's, who will give you that which is your own?"_ Stewardship of our finances says a lot regarding our spirituality. Let me see a man's checkbook, and in a few minutes I can tell you his priorities and values. The implication of this passage is that how we use money has something to do with what spiritual blessings God can entrust to us.

The fourth dimension of stewardship is an area that often is omitted in sermons on the subject. Most of us have given little thought to this, but God calls every believer also to be a good steward of **truth.**

📖 Look at 2 Timothy 2:2.

What is the treasure Paul is calling Timothy to manage wisely?

_____

_____

In what kind of person is Timothy to invest truth?

_____

_____

_____

Word Study
ENTRUST

In 2 Timothy 2:2, Paul calls us to "entrust" truth. The Greek word that is translated "entrust" is *paratithēmi* (par-at-ith'-ay-mee), which means to place alongside, i.e. present (food, truth) by implication, to deposit (as a trust or for protection).

God, through His servants, has invested truth in every believer. Perhaps some of us know more than others, but all of us have received some truth, and 2 Timothy 2:2 speaks loudly to this issue as Paul exhorts Timothy: *"The things which you have heard from me . . . these entrust to faithful men, who will be able to teach others also."*

Each of us has seen truth modeled and heard it taught. This truth thus becomes in our lives a treasure to be managed, a stewardship to be entrusted to others who will then do the same with still others—and the Christian faith grows and spreads. This directive is echoed in the Great Commission recorded in Matthew 28:18–20. Christ commands us to be *"teaching them to observe all that I commanded you."*

We are stewards of all that God has built into our lives, and we will one day give an account to Him. Knowing this helps me in my decision-making. At times it may mean saying no to temporal opportunities in favor of eternal ones. Being a faithful steward of God's truth may mean I don't climb the corporate ladder as fast or as high as others whose only commitment is to the company or to themselves. God's will for me may not mean I'm the top salesman or the youngest junior partner, but whatever it does mean will be good, and acceptable, and perfect (see Romans 12:2).

CARPOOL SIGN
Day Four
STEWARDSHIP

CARPOOL LANE

WHAT IS REQUIRED OF A STEWARD?

Each of us is a steward; that is already settled. The question of the Christian life, then, is, What kind of steward am I? Since Scripture makes it certain that one day I will give an account to God for my life, the admonition of 1 Corinthians 4:2 ought to ring loudly in my ears: *"Moreover, it is required of stewards that one be found trustworthy."* If I am a trustworthy steward, if I have been found faithful, I will be rewarded.

📖 Look at 1 Corinthians 3:10–15. What are the different outcomes of faithfulness verses unfaithfulness?

_____

_____

_____

_____

If I am faithful, I will be rewarded. Some think the gold, silver, and precious jewels are the very materials used to make our crowns. If I am unfaithful, my salvation is still secure, but my reward is forfeited, and I will *"suffer loss."* In other words, it will be worth it to be faithful to the Lord.

📖 Read Galatians 2:20–21 and write what you learn about stewardship.

_____

_____

_____

_____

_____

When I became a Christian, I died to the old, selfish manner of living. Christ now lives in me and desires to live through me. If that desire is realized, He will make the choices on what to do with my blessings.

📖 What do you learn in Romans 14:7–9 about being a good steward?

_____

_____

_____

_____

_____

The message could not be clearer: we are not to live self-centered lives. Christ did not free us from the bondage of sin to then become enslaved to self.

Some Dangers of Misapplication

Stewardship is one way God guides me in the decision of life, but it comes with a warning. In order for stewardship to be effective in my decisions, I must be operating on an eternal value system. I must place the highest premium on the things that are important to God and that will last in eternity. Otherwise my scales of decision will be unbalanced. If I weigh temporal values such as pleasure, success, achievement, etc., too heavily, then I will draw wrong conclusions about God's leading. Stewardship speaks with the voice and values of God, and if His values are not mine, my going will not be with His guiding.

FOR ME TO HEAR GOD

Every one of us is a steward of some kind. We may be a good one or a bad one, but either way we are a steward. Because God has entrusted some of His blessings to us, He has made us stewards, and He calls us to faithful management of the things that belong to Him. Maybe this is a new idea for you. Or maybe it is an idea that has expanded in your understanding through this week's lesson. Remember that you are accountable for this knowledge.

Did You Know?
CROWNS

The Bible speaks of our rewards as coming in the form of crowns. There are four specific crowns mentioned in the New Testament: The crown of glory (1 Peter 5:4), the imperishable crown (1 Corinthians 9:25), the crown of righteousness (2 Timothy 4:8), and the crown of life (James 1:12). Revelation 4:10 seems to indicate that we will use these crowns to worship Jesus in heaven as we lay them at His feet.

CARPOOL SIGN

Day Five

STEWARDSHIP

As you consider the different areas of stewardship, evaluate how you think you are doing in each area. (Place an "X" in the appropriate location on the line.)

Stewardship of your time

Faithful ◄————— 1 ——— 2 ——— 3 ——— 4 ——— 5 —————► Unfaithful

Stewardship of your talents

Faithful ◄————— 1 ——— 2 ——— 3 ——— 4 ——— 5 —————► Unfaithful

Stewardship of your treasures

Faithful ◄————— 1 ——— 2 ——— 3 ——— 4 ——— 5 —————► Unfaithful

Stewardship of your truth

Faithful ◄————— 1 ——— 2 ——— 3 ——— 4 ——— 5 —————► Unfaithful

Each person is a steward; that is already settled. The question of the Christian life, then, is, "What kind of steward am I?"

What do you sense you need to be doing differently?

As we saw in Steve's decision to go into ministry instead of business, stewardship can be one of the ways God speaks His will. Evaluate your decision in light of how it reflects your stewardship of these four key areas of your life, and apply the **CARPOOL** signpost to your decision-making process:

Stewardship of your **time**

_____

_____

_____

Stewardship of your **talents**

_____

_____

_____

Stewardship of your **treasures**

_____

_____

_____

Stewardship of your **truth**

_____

_____

_____

Why not close out this week's lesson with a written prayer of surrender. Express your heart to God and let Him know your desire to be a faithful steward.

_____

_____

_____

_____

_____

_____

_____

_____

_____

_____

Notes

THE "NO PARKING" SIGN:
Faith

"Lord, am I missing Your will?" I quietly prayed. "I know that if I turn from Your will, I am turning to a lie, so what should I do, Lord?" As I stammered out these silent supplications, my heart reeled in turmoil. It was the culmination of weeks of agonizing about a decision I had made two months earlier. I had decided to leave my position directing Campus Crusade's ministry at the University of Tennessee and accept a job as an associate pastor of a church. I handed in my resignation over Christmas to give time for a replacement to be found, and I was finishing out the school year. With so much time to think about it, I began to wonder if I had made the right decision.

After working with Campus Crusade for Christ for more than six years, I felt that God wanted to move me on. I had committed to the Lord, however, that I would not leave my present ministry and go to something else without a clear sense of calling from Him. I like the way Major Ian Thomas puts it: "If you were SENT, and you WENT, then you are PUT." In other words, if you had a call and you obeyed it, then there is no need to change anything until you get a new call.

It seemed that the direction I was heading and the decision I had made were following the leading of God. But I had second

"If you were SENT, and you WENT, then you are PUT."
—Major Ian Thomas

thoughts—major secondthoughts. I feared the consequences of leaving God's will, but I was so far along in the process, I couldn't back out now. My house was up for sale. My job had been assigned to someone else for the next year. I had told all my friends confidently I was following God in leaving the staff and moving to a church. I was also anxious about stepping from a significant ministry into an unknown area of church work. Was I really following God? Or was I just tired of walking by faith? Had I been lured away from God's leading by the promise of a steady salary I didn't have to raise? How did I get to this point?

As I hung my head in a humble spirit of prayer, I thought back over the events of the past year that had brought me to this place. I had always desired to work in a local church and long suspected that my gifts of teaching and leading were better suited for that service, and the past summer that desire deepened and became more defined. As a culmination to books I read, prayers I prayed, and Scriptures I studied, God began to give me a specific vision for my life. I was convinced that the world would not be reached for Christ with so little of our Christian manpower tapped. I was frustrated and burdened by the great number of Christians in local churches across America whose faith is largely a spectator sport. In the average local church only about five percent of the people have a personal ministry.

As God began to knit these perspectives and passions together, I began asking Him to open the door for me to move to the local church. I began praying for an opportunity to be a part of a new reformation of local churches moving people toward ministry. I began trusting God to put me in a situation where I not only could have a local ministry but also could serve as a catalyst to other churches.

About this time a pastor friend named Wayne Barber contacted me regarding a position at his church. Whenever I had thought about local church ministry, I often though of brother Wayne. I had met him five years earlier and liked him immediately. He was a strong and gifted expository teacher of the Scriptures. In fact, he was the principle male teacher alongside Kay Arthur for Precept Ministries, an international Bible-teaching outreach.

Wayne's church was as close as any I had ever seen to what I believe the biblical model to be. He and I thought so much alike, and we dreamed so much alike. In fact, just after I first met him I asked the Lord to let me serve with him some day.

My call from Wayne was made by the right person, at the right place, during the right time. The only problem was that the position Wayne offered did not seem to be the right position. He asked me to consider coming as youth pastor for junior high through college age rather than in the area of evangelism and discipleship, a position I was believing God for but which they already had filled. It wasn't what I expected.

I knew I could relate with the college students, but I wasn't so sure about the high schoolers, and I was scared to death at the thought of junior highers. Would I be able to relate with them? Would I really be able to minister? To be honest, I was disappointed. But I so wanted to work with Wayne, and I did feel God was leading me to the local church. Maybe this was His way of moving me toward where He ultimately wanted me to be.

"Now that no one is justified by the Law before God is evident; for, 'The righteous man shall live by faith.'"

Galatians 3:11

After much prayer, I concluded that this was in fact what He wanted me to do, and He would make me adequate for the task. And then, sooner or later, He would turn my ministry in the direction of discipleship and evangelism. All I needed at that time was to step out in faith and trust Him to work things out His way. So I did. I accepted the position, and I handed my resignation into Campus Crusade.

But, as I said, now I wasn't so sure. This nagging sense of doubt dulled my zeal and clouded my thoughts. In my mind, the title "Youth Pastor" sounded so insignificant, like stepping aside from the real cause of Christ to babysit. "What should I do, Lord?"

Minute after agonizing minute went by as I finally came to the point of complete surrender. "Lord, whatever You want me to do, I'll do it. If You want me to ask for my old job back, I'll do it. If I can't get it back, I'll trust You with it. Whatever You want, Lord, just show me."

I sat silently, half-expecting God to confirm that I had missed His will. Instead, He began bringing to my mind the many ways He had already confirmed His leading. Soon I realized I already knew God's will, even if I didn't fully understand it. I just needed to keep walking by faith.

THE FAITH PRINCIPLE

The next sign we encounter on the way to God's will is the **NO PARKING** sign. One of the overriding principles of the Christian life is that it is a walk of faith. This is especially significant in determining God's will. Many times God asks us to take a step of faith before He shows us what He is up to. Often, further revelation of His will follows when we have taken the steps of faith equivalent to His present leading.

One of our biggest dangers is parking by sight instead of moving by faith. In the Christian life, sometimes God slows us down by telling us to wait, but we should never park.

📖 There are several passages in the New Testament which, when woven together, show us what faith is from a practical perspective. Look at the verses below and write what you learn there about living by faith.

Galatians 3:11

_____

_____

_____

_____

Hebrews 11:6

_____

_____

_____

_____

_____

_____

_____

Faith is a fundamental of the Christian life. Galatians 3:11 makes it clear that living by faith is a righteous thing. God wants us to live by faith. Hebrews 11:6 makes it clear that it is impossible to please God without faith. This verse points out two paramount principles of what faith is. First, faith is believing that God is—that He exists, and that He is who the Scriptures say He is. Second, faith is trusting that God rewards those who seek Him. When we understand this, we will want to involve Him in every area of our lives. Romans 14:23 shows us the flip side of faith—whatever is not flowing out of faith is sin.

📖 Look at Jeremiah 17:5–8 and identify the consequences of trusting in God compared with the consequences of trusting in man.

_____

_____

_____

_____

_____

Trusting in God brings blessing, while trusting in man brings curse. Sooner or later man will always disappoint us and let us down. God is not that way. Trusting in man is like being a bush in the desert—dependent on inconsistent rain to have our needs met. Trusting in God is like being a tree planted by a continual source of water. If we are to experience the life God has for us, it will be only by faith—trusting Him step by step.

Sometimes the way to where God is leading us is not "as the crow flies." Discerning God's will is not merely figuring out where He wants us, but following as He leads us. His leading may involve detours. It may involve rest stops. He may even take us aside to teach us and to prepare us for where He will lead later.

You see, God's will is not a **point,** but a **process.**

"NO PARKING" SIGN

Day Two

FAITH

GOD'S WILL IS A PROCESS

The process of a Christian walk can be broken down and dissected into specific points. It is a process of learning, a process of growing, a process not simply of doing, but of becoming. Many times we make the mistake of seeking God's will only in the major decision, the crisis points. But effectiveness at these times is linked to the ongoing process of following Christ in everyday things.

Note the words of Proverbs 3:5–6: *"Trust in the LORD with all your heart, and do not lean on your own understanding. In all your ways acknowledge Him, and He will make your paths straight."* Here, Solomon describes this principle of God's will as being a process rather than just a point.

Do you notice the repetition of the word **all**? Major decisions are much more difficult when we haven't involved God in the minor ones. *"Trust in the LORD with* **all** *your heart"* indicates a relationship, not simply instructions to follow. *"In* **all** *your ways acknowledge Him"* reflects the fact that following God in the minor decision makes us more receptive to Him in the major ones. When we trust and acknowledge the Lord, we have the promise that *"He will make* [our] *paths straight* [clear or right]." Major decisions will not become major headaches.

I like the way Paul Little expresses this principle of process in his booklet *Affirming the Will of God* (Downers Grove, IL: InterVarsity Press, 1999). Let's look at it again:

> *The will of God is not like a magic package let down from heaven by a string. . . . the will of God is far more like a scroll that unrolls every day. . . .the will of God is something to be discerned and lived out every day of our lives. It is not something to be grasped as a package once for all. Our call, therefore, is basically not to follow a plan or a blueprint, or to go to a place or take up a work, but rather to follow the Lord Jesus Christ.*

If we seek God's will only at the crisis points, why even bother? Of what value can His leading be in the major decisions if we have not followed His wisdom in the minor ones?

Why God's Will Is a Process

Why do you think God makes His will a process? Why doesn't He just hand out road maps and send us on our way?

The answer is complex but not complicated.

First of all, think about your own life. What would it be like if you knew right now where God wanted you to be in twenty years? How would such knowledge affect the here and now? If you are like me, knowing the future would make it much harder to live in the present. I would be tempted to take shortcuts. For example, if I knew at age 20 whom God wanted me to marry, why bother dating anyone else? Yet dating other people helped me to become who I needed to be in my marriage. If I knew before I took a job that it was a dead end, would I still take it? How would I have learned the lessons I needed without that process? If I knew before I ran a race that I would lose, would I still run? If we knew the end from the beginning, **it would be all too easy to let our "logic" supersede God's leading.**

Can you think of some examples in Scripture of this?

_____

_____

_____

_____

_____

God's will is not a point, but a process.

"The will of God . . . is not something to be grasped as a package once for all. Our call, therefore, is basically not to follow a plan or a blueprint, or to go to a place or take up a work, but rather to follow the Lord Jesus Christ."

—Paul Little
Affirming the Will of God
InterVarsity Press, 1999

_____

_____

_____

Another reason God's will is a process is that **tomorrow's assignments cannot be handled with today's faith.** If I knew that tomorrow held martyrdom for me, would I be able to take the steps today that lead to that path? Today's process builds my faith for tomorrow's assignments. It is faithfulness in the little things today that makes me sturdy enough to be faithful in the big things tomorrow.

📖 Look at Matthew 6:34. How does God direct us to trust Him?

_____

_____

_____

_____

In the Sermon on the Mount, Jesus said, *"Do not be anxious for tomorrow; for tomorrow will care for itself. Each day has enough trouble of its own."* It is enough to trust God for today—He is not going to give me the faith for tomorrow until tomorrow comes. I think this attitude must have been what He was getting at. Remember: How do you walk a mile? One step at a time. There is no other way.

Understanding this reality of God's will being a process enabled me to say yes to a detour and to accept a job that didn't seem in line with my long-term direction. But my commitment to the process of God's will also caused me to have second thoughts. None of us is always on track. None of us makes all the right decisions. None of us ever avoids excursions into sin. That is why God's will must be a process—**it allows imperfect people to keep coming back.**

"NO PARKING" SIGN

Day Three

FAITH

YOU HAVE TO KEEP MOVING

As I sought God in the middle of my process, He confirmed that I was on the right track. I just needed to keep trusting and keep moving. This underscores one of the big dangers we spoke of earlier— "parking." Have you ever done it? I have, many times.

We sit back and look for everything to work out before we go any further. The problem is, if you are sitting in a parked car, it is hard to know which way your tires are turned. But once you start moving, you know which way they are headed and you can make corrections if necessary. Following God is like that. Sometimes it takes a step of faith to see which way we are heading, but once we do, we see more clearly where we are to go.

It is also easier to turn the steering wheel once the car is moving. Following God is a lot like that. It is much easier for Him to redirect us if we are moving than to turn us if we are standing still. This is another indication that following God's will is a process. I had to shift out of park and get moving.

When I did, and I became willing to veer from my course toward the church position, God confirmed that I was on the right course after all.

What about you? Is your car in park or in gear? If the process of God's will seems to be at an impasse in your life, maybe it's because you aren't moving.

One of the ways we learn to trust God is from the example of others. Today we want to examine a biblical example of this important principle of walking by faith.

📖 Read through 1 Samuel 17. What was David's faith situation? (17:23)

_____

_____

_____

David did not go to visit his brothers expecting to be used by God in a national way. He was merely bringing a care package from home. Yet he suddenly found himself in a faith situation. As he heard the Philistine giant, Goliath, mocking God, his spirit was stirred within him. If Jesus is the author of faith, then we can assume that the ability to trust God with Goliath didn't originate with David. David would have to go into battle, but God was the initiator of the situation.

📖 What were David's possible feelings and fears? (17:26–34)

_____

_____

_____

_____

David had ample reason to fear the situation. He was a young man with no military experience. Every indication we have in Scripture is that David was a small man. Goliath, on the other hand, was a giant. Goliath was also a veteran soldier. Physically, David was no match for Goliath, and he could not trust in himself to win the battle.

What past examples of God's sufficiency did David draw on? (17:34–37)

_____

_____

_____

This was not the first faith situation David had faced. In his work as a shepherd boy, he had twice before encountered an enemy too great for his own strength. He had fought both a lion and a bear and come away victorious. David recognized that it was God who worked through him in such situations. He said, _"The Lord who delivered me . . . will deliver me. . . ."_

On what aspects of God's character did David focus? (17:45–46)

_____

_____

_____

As David approached Goliath, he did so with recognition that Jehovah was *"the LORD of hosts."* This term meant God of the armies of heaven. God is also called *"the God of the armies of Israel."* The Hebrew word for *"LORD"* here is *"Yahweh"* or *"Jehovah,"* and the Hebrew word for "God" is *"Elohim."* David trusted God's power as he went down to face Goliath.

📖 What action did David take? (17:45–49)

_____

_____

_____

_____

Although David trusted God, he clearly had a part in the battle. He went down into the valley to encounter Goliath. He ran to the battle line. He placed a stone in his sling and set it in motion. He used the weapon he knew how to use, and he trusted God to energize his effort and make it effective.

Faith is not just trusting God to work, but it is trusting Him to work through us. Walking by faith is not parking and waiting for God to do for us what we will not do ourselves. Waiting on God is sometimes an act of faith, but we have to be careful that it does not become an act of walking by sight.

"NO PARKING" SIGN

Day Four

FAITH

BARRIERS TO DOING GOD'S WILL

The principal hindrance in the process of following God is that we tend to pull away from leading that requires a step of faith. It is easier to say yes to something that appeals to my flesh than something that appeals to my spirit, because following God involves taking steps of faith, and my flesh doesn't like that. Paul puts it this way: *"we walk by faith, not by sight"* (2 Corinthians 5:7). Walking by sight means I can figure out all the angles; everything makes sense; everything fits. Walking by faith means trusting God even if I can't figure out all the angles, even if nothing makes sense—but my flesh doesn't like to do that. What about your flesh?

When we consider the barriers to walking by faith, I see two main ones: fear of failure, and a lack of biblical knowledge. With fear of failure, I think every person has a "comfort zone" or a risk threshhold. God sometimes calls us to move beyond that into areas where we are not comfortable. Since the righteous shall live by faith, God is going to put us in situations that require it. Sometimes our struggles with faith are rooted in not having enough truth from which to operate. Let's look at some scriptural solutions to these problems.

Look at the verses listed and see how they address the fear of failure as a barrier.

Philippians 4:13

_____

_____

_____

"We walk by faith, not by sight."

2 Corinthians 5:7

Ephesians 3:16

_____

_____

_____

_____

2 Corinthians 12:9–10

_____

_____

_____

_____

These verses are some healthy reminders when we struggle with trusting God. We <u>can</u> do all things through Him who strengthens us. Ephesians tells us God can strengthen us with power in the inner man (inner power). Perhaps most encouraging is the example of Paul. Even he had weaknesses, but he learned that it was in those areas that he most experienced the power of Christ. He actually came to a place where he could boast of his weaknesses! We can too.

📖 Look up the references listed below and see how they address lack of biblical knowledge as a barrier.

Romans 10:17

_____

_____

_____

_____

2 Timothy 2:15

_____

_____

_____

_____

2 Timothy 3:16–17

_____

_____

_____

_____

Hebrews 4:12

_____

_____

_____

_____

Romans 10:17 is one of the most important verses on walking by faith. It tells us that faith comes by hearing and hearing by the Word of God. In other words, reading and studying and hearing the Word of God makes it easier to trust Him. The more we know, the easier faith becomes. In 2 Timothy 2:15 we are exhorted to be diligent in handling the Word accurately. Sometimes our faith is eroded not because we aren't in the Word, but because we aren't handling it right. Second Timothy 3:16–17 shows us how the Word can help us, and it reminds us that it is the Word which equips us to do the work God calls us to. In Hebrews 4:12 we are reminded that the Word can help us by judging the thoughts and intentions of the heart.

If, like me, you sometimes struggle with taking steps of faith, perhaps the conclusion of my story will be an encouragement to you. Even though it didn't all make sense, I headed toward the church job by faith. I just had to trust that in time the vision and burden God had given me would come to pass.

I finished my ministry at the University of Tennessee about the second week of May and then packed my family up for a vacation before starting my new job. Several days into our vacation I got a phone call from my boss-to-be, Wayne Barber. The fellow they had hired as Associate Pastor of Discipleship became increasingly frustrated with his job description. He didn't have the vision or desire for discipleship. What he really enjoyed was working with young people. He had served for a number of years as youth pastor at another church. Not knowing where my heart was, Wayne called to see if I would consider trading job descriptions with the other man. When I climbed down from the ceiling, I give him an enthusiastic "yes!" God knew all along how things would work out. I just had to trust Him while He clued everyone else in.

The process God took me through taught me much about discerning His will. One of the results is this book, but it is not only the fruit of that process—it is part of the process. One of my desires has been to be a catalyst for others in their journey of faith and to engage in ministry outside my church. Getting this book published is a part of that. I haven't found God's will for my life yet—I'm still following it.

FOR ME TO HEAR GOD

W hat about you? Does this idea of following God's will, instead of just finding it, meet you where you are? God's will is a journey that we will continue until He returns or calls us home. That journey will be walked by faith, not sight. Christianity is more than a religion, it is a relationship with the living God. But since He is spirit and we are flesh, that relationship must be lived by the faith principle. Without faith, it is impossible to please Him. What is not of faith, is sin. We must walk by faith, not sight. The righteous will live by faith. These are not just ideas, they are Scriptures—truth given to us from God. We cannot have a meaningful relationship with Him if we are not willing to trust Him. That choice to trust is what the Bible calls faith. That faith is a lot like a muscle—it develops with use, and deteriorates without it. As we have looked at the "No Parking" sign this week, we have much to apply to our own lives and decisions.

Considering each of the following questions and recording your answers will help you apply the signpost of faith to your pursuit of God and His will.

 Look at the categories listed in the chart below on the left. Evaluate yourself as to whether you tend to walk in each category by faith or by sight by placing a checkmark in the appropriate box.

AREA	WALK BY FAITH	WALK BY SIGHT
Finances		
Family		
Employment		
Accomplishments		
Friendships		
Recreation		
Giving		
Serving		
Time Management		
Other		

Faith is a lot like a muscle—it develops with use, and deteriorates without it. The more we exercise that muscle, the more that muscle is able to accomplish.

As you consider your own struggles with walking by sight instead of faith, what role does fear of failure play in that struggle?

_____
_____
_____
_____
_____

What role does lack of biblical knowledge play?

_____
_____
_____
_____

Hopefully, as you have been working through this study, you have had in mind a decision in which you can apply these principles. Consider the questions below as you seek to make that application.

What steps of faith does God want me to take in my present decision and circumstances?

_____
_____
_____
_____

> *"And without faith it is impossible to please Him, for he who comes to God must believe that He is, and that He is a rewarder of those who seek Him."*
>
> Hebrews 11:6

What steps of faith am I trying to avoid?

_____

_____

_____

_____

What specific areas or circumstances in this decision do I have to trust God to work out?

_____

_____

_____

_____

A Prayer

Dear Lord, I want to walk by faith in this decision and not by sight or self-effort. Help me to trust You and lean on You. Make me sensitive to any area I am not trusting You with and help me to obey. Amen.

You may want to write your own prayer to the Lord in the space below. . .

_____

_____

_____

_____

_____

_____

_____

_____

_____

Notes

Notes

THE "STOP" SIGN:
Waiting

"Do you think we will ever be able to buy a house?" my wife asked in painful honesty. We had moved to town a few months earlier and were no closer to finding a house we could afford and could fit into than when we first moved. When I accepted the church job, Michele made many trips down to our hometown-to-be. She had grown up there and already knew which areas were safe and livable and which were not. After several months of looking, she still hadn't found anything acceptable in our price range. We weren't worried, though, and decided to rent a house until we sold our old home.

A couple from our new church had a house for sale, and they offered to rent it to us on a month-by-month basis if we were willing to let them leave it on the market. It was located conveniently close to my work, and they gave us a break on the price, so it seemed like a good deal. But the months ticked by and we still couldn't find a permanent home. We became increasingly nervous knowing that at any time someone might buy the house we were renting, and then where would we be?

I think this time of looking and waiting was hardest on my wife. A home she is happy with is so important to a woman. The months

"Wait for the LORD; Be strong, and let your heart take courage; Yes, wait for the LORD.
Psalm 27:14

of living out of boxes and the continual frustration of looking and finding nothing took their toll. We knew God had called us to be there, and we continued to seek His wisdom and to ask Him to provide, but nothing happened.

Finally, we had a breakthrough. A contractor friend offered to build us a home at a substantial discount. If we could find an acceptable lot in our price range, our new home would immediately be worth more than we paid for it. It took a while, but eventually we stumbled across half-a-dozen lots of which a bank had foreclosed. They were in our price range and only a few miles from my work. It seemed God had provided at last!

The next few weeks were a whirlwind of activity as we settled on a set of plans, looked at finances, and arranged for the contractor to do the final survey of the lot to make sure everything was okay. Then the snags began. First, a limitation in the building code of the subdivision required a concrete driveway instead of asphalt. Chi-ching! The cash register rang out—the cost had gone up. Then we had to agree to a 70-percent brick exterior. Chi-ching! The cost went up some more.

And then there was the extra grading work and the septic tank. Chi-ching!

The straw that broke our financial camel's back came from the water company. The first one hundred feet of water line were free, but there was a small problem. Ours was the last lot on the street, and in order for us to get water service, we would have pay to run the water line across four empty lots, to the tune of $3,500. Part of this money would be refunded when (and if) the other lots were built on, but we didn't have that kind of money to flex with.

We had to admit that the dream house in our price range wasn't in our price range anymore. My wife's grandparents offered to loan us the difference and give us a couple of years to start paying on it, but the more we prayed about it, the more we became convinced that we were the ones making things happen, not God. We could find no rest in our spirits. We were striving and finagling rather than seeing God answer our prayers.

Finally, after several late-night conversations in bed, my wife and I agreed that building on the lot we'd found was not God's way of meeting our needs. But what was? Sooner or later we would have to find a permanent home. What was the Lord trying to tell us?

Word Study
WAIT

The Hebrew word usually translated "wait" (*qâwâh*) literally means "to bind together by twisting." The picture that is painted emphasizes the process of weaving things together—In other words, patience with the time it takes for the weaving to be completed. Waiting on God is an acknowledgement that He is weaving circumstances and situations together and that He is not going to give us everything we want when we want it, but rather, when we need it.

STOP SIGN
Day One
WAITING

WAIT TRAINING

The next signpost we come to as we travel down this road to God's will is the **STOP** sign. Sometimes as we seek God's will, instead of giving us the answer we desire, God says, "Wait." Have you ever experienced that? This is where Michele and I found ourselves at that time. It seemed every direction we turned offered another brick wall. Perhaps no signpost is more difficult to accept gracefully than this one, but the only time we experienced God's peace was when we waited.

In America convenience is king. When we want instant breakfast, we just add milk. Dinner goes from the freezer to the microwave to the table in less than ten minutes. When we need instant cash, we have automated teller machines available twenty-four hours a day. If we want a letter to go overnight, we Federal Express it, and if that isn't fast enough, we fax or e-mail it. From coast-to-coast jet travel to quick-dry nail polish, there is little in our culture that cultivates patience. Yet God quite often calls us to wait. As I read through the Psalms, I am amazed at how many times that annoying word *wait* appears. I think God is trying to tell us something.

David was a man acquainted with waiting. Even though he was anointed king as a young lad, it would be years before he would actually take the throne.

📖 Look at 1 Samuel 16:1–14 and meditate on God's calling of David as King, making note of anything that stands out to you.

_____

_____

_____

_____

_____

It is clear from this passage that it was God, not David, who initiated him being king. It was not because of David's credentials that he was selected, nor was it because of his accomplishments. Verse 7 makes it clear that the primary thing God was looking for was the heart, and in David He found *"a man after His own heart"* (verse 7).

📖 Now read 1 Samuel 16:14—23:29 and overview the major events listed there that precede David's actually becoming king. This will take a little time, so feel free to skim through it, but it will be worth it to actually see in the Scriptures the process of waiting God had in store for David.

_____

_____

_____

_____

_____

_____

David recognized that it was not his job, but God's to make him king.

A lot happens between David's anointing as king and his actually taking the throne. You probably didn't realize that David's encounter with Goliath was after the prophet Samuel had anointed him. This was followed by his friendship with Saul's son, Jonathan, and his service to Saul. Early on, David had a good relationship with Saul, but soon jealousy and fear turned Saul against him. Twice David barely escaped with his life (18:11). Repeatedly, Saul sent David into battle, hoping to do him harm, but God was with David. When that didn't work, Saul in effect put a bounty on his head (chapter 19). David even delivered the city of Keilah from the Philistines, only to have Saul come war against him there. Thus began years of hiding and running—with Saul in hot pursuit. Saul had been rejected as king, but he was trying to keep the throne through striving.

📖 Look at 1 Samuel 24:1–4. With what opportunity is David presented to secure his kingship?

_____

_____

_____

_____

_____

An interesting event occurs here. Saul had tried again and again to kill David, but he had been unsuccessful. That alone would be a culturally accepted motive for David to kill Saul. It would be viewed as self-defense. Not only that, but Saul held the throne that the prophet Samuel had already promised to David. He knew that it was God's will for him to be king. No one in Israel would have blamed David for getting Saul out of the way. When Saul unknowingly comes into the very cave where David is hiding, revenge is within David's grasp if he desires.

📖 Identify David's response in 1 Samuel 24:5–6 and write your observations about how this reflects an attitude of waiting on God.

_____

_____

_____

Instead of killing Saul (who would certainly have killed him if the roles were reversed) David cuts off the edge of his robe as proof of what he could have done. Verse 6 is significant. David refused to take matters into his own hands, and make himself king. If he were to take the throne, he wanted it through God's enabling, not man's. He was waiting on God to work. This attitude is expressed more fully in verse 12: _"May the LORD judge between you and me, and may the LORD avenge me on you; but my hand shall not be against you."_

So complete was David's waiting on God, that he even spared Saul a second time when he could have killed him (1 Samuel 26). David's attitude was _"As the LORD lives, surely the LORD will strike him, or his day will come that he dies, or he will go down into battle and perish. The LORD forbid that I should stretch out my hand against the LORD'S anointed"_ (26:10–11). David's expectation was soon fulfilled, for Saul died in a battle with the Philistines (1 Samuel 31). So great was David's respect for the office of king that he grieved when Saul died. He had waited on the Lord, and the Lord finally made him king.

"May the LORD judge between you and me, and may the LORD avenge me on you; but my hand shall not be against you."

(David, speaking to King Saul)

1 Samuel 24:12

STOP | **Day Two**

STOP SIGN

WAITING

Why Wait?

Ours is a culture which values the "self-made man." We expect men to climb the ladder of success, and we applaud them when they do. "When the going gets tough, the tough get going" is one of our favorite mottos. In this kind of climate, waiting on God is sometimes viewed as pacivity. But waiting is not passive; it is active. It is choosing not to do something, because we sense the Lord is saying "wait." If we are to follow God or hear God, we must be sensitive to His Spirit and discern when we are to step out in faith and when we are to wait.

📖 Look at Psalm 37.

What are some evidences that we are not "waiting on the Lord" in our hearts (verse 1)?

_____

_____

_____

_____

What needs to come before the Lord will give us the desires of our hearts (verses 3–5)?

_____

_____

_____

_____

What actions are contrasted with waiting on the Lord (verses 7–9)?

_____

_____

_____

_____

> *"Rest in the LORD and wait patiently for Him."*
>
> **Psalm 37:7**

Fretting and being envious are evidences that we are not really waiting in our hearts, according to verse 1. What God desires is that we would delight in Him. These verses list a lot of practical things we must do before God will give us what we are seeking. We must trust Him, and we must do good. We are called to delight in Him so that He can begin to shape our desires. We need to commit our way to Him, and let Him do it. The central call of this chapter is in verse 7: *"rest in the Lord and wait patiently for Him."* Some actions that reflect our impatience are reflected in feelings like fretting, anger, and wrath.

Psalm 37:7 says, *"Rest in the Lord and wait patiently for Him."* But why? I believe there are many reasons God sends us through "wait training." We need to learn lessons there that cannot be learned anywhere else. When we seek God and His answer seems to be "wait," we don't always hear it because that answer is not the one we are seeking. Michele and I wanted to move into a home, so we weren't always content when God's answer was "wait," but He used the process to keep us seeking Him.

One of the lessons God teaches us in "wait training" is to **keep our eyes on Him, not on our circumstances.** One of the real blessings for my wife and me during our nine months of renting was learning that we could experience God's peace and rest even if our circumstances weren't as we liked. When we wait on God for something, that area serves as a continual reminder to keep our eyes on Jesus, something we are always called to do.

📖 Look at Psalm 46.

Verse 1 reminds us that God is our refuge and strength and help in trouble. What kind of trouble is taking place in verses 2–9?

_____

_____

_____

What is our response when we are in the midst of similar circumstances (see verse 10)?

_____

_____

_____

God desires that we take refuge in Him in the midst of our troubles. Look at the context of this passage: catastrophe is going on. The earth is changing; the mountains are crumbling; and the rivers are overflowing. In such situations the temptation is to run around putting Band-Aids on everything, but God desires that we would quit striving and recognize Him in the midst of our circumstances.

Another lesson we learn in waiting is that **the giver is more important than the gift.** A child who always gets what he wants when he wants it is not a grateful child and ultimately isn't happy. Waiting helps us put life in perspective, and often it causes us to come to grips with what we have rather than bemoaning what we don't have.

📖 Look at James 1:17. What is the message there about the source of gifts?

_____

_____

_____

As we look to the Lord for answers, for provision, we realize who He is, and we see that ultimately, _"Every good thing bestowed and every perfect gift is from above"_ (James 1:17). When we wait for something, we appreciate it when it is given, and we also learn to appreciate the one who gives it.

A third thing waiting teaches us is, **there is a difference between needs and wants.** When God calls us to wait, He also calls us to do without for a time. In these times of deprivation, we learn what our limits are and what we are capable of handling as human beings. I have known great times of financial blessing; and I have known great times of scarcity; and to be honest, I didn't learn much from the blessings. I grew more as a person and as a Christian during adversity than I ever grew in any time of abundance. When we say we "need" a second car, what we really mean is we "want" one. When we say we "need" a bigger house, what we really mean is we "want" one. I'm not saying God never gives us our wants—He has blessed me in immeasurable ways—but part of maturity is learning the difference between what I need and what I want. Waiting teaches me that.

"Cease striving and know that I am God; I will be exalted among the nations, I will be exalted in the earth."

Psalm 46:10

📖 Read 1 Timothy 6:6–10 and summarize the message.

_____

_____

_____

_____

What God desires from us is that we are willing to be content with what He trusts to us. All we really NEED is our daily bread and a place to lay our head. The sad reality is that all the toys we try to accumulate in this life are not eternal, and therefore, are eternally insignificant.

Finally, **waiting demonstrates faith in God instead of in ourselves.** This is the message when Psalm 46 tells us to _"cease striving."_ You see, waiting is a choice. It is a decision that says, "I want what God provides." It is a result of volition. It is believing that what God provides is better than what I can do by myself, and surrendering to that. When Michele and I first began looking for a home, we already knew it would be a long-term decision. Barring the Lord's intervention, I expect to be where I am for some time to come. It will take years for my dreams and vision to be realized. Knowing this, we didn't want to settle for a home we would later regret. So we committed to the Lord to wait for what He provided—and I believe He took so long in granting our request for a home to test our level of faith and commitment. Waiting is an act of faith.

What about you? Are you waiting on the Lord in your decision? If you aren't, you will find yourself making things happen on your own, and you will ultimately settle for second best. An old saying, popular where I come from, goes like this: "You can have hamburgers at five o'clock or steak at seven." Things worth waiting for usually require waiting. In job choices, in mate choices, in life choices, I have seen people settle for less than the best because they weren't willing to wait. If I am unwilling to wait for God's will, that is what I will forfeit—His will. If I want the _"good and acceptable and perfect will of God,"_ I will probably be called to wait for it.

> _If I want the good, acceptable, perfect will of God, I will probably be called to wait for it._

Some Key Principles

STOP SIGN
Day Three
WAITING

O ne key principle we must understand about waiting is that God's ways and our ways are different.

📖 Look at Isaiah 55:8–9 and summarize its message.

_____

_____

_____

_____

God doesn't think the way we think, and His way of doing things is different too. God's timing is not necessarily the same as ours. Even knowing that something is God's will does not mean it is His time. God has a higher way of doing things, and everything He does operates from total knowledge and total power. We can trust the way He does what He does. Waiting is a practical way we express that trust.

Joseph knew early in life that one day his brothers would bow down to him (see Genesis 37:5–12), and I'm sure he sometimes got impatient for that to come about. However, God had much preparation work to do in Joseph's life before he could be exalted in this manner. It took years of waiting before Joseph's dream was realized.

And David—he could have taken a shortcut to the throne by killing King Saul when he had the chance, but it wouldn't have been God's way. The Lord would not have been glorified in it. We must recognize that the way God accomplishes His will may take much longer than our method would take. This principle was crucial to the process we went through in buying a house. We could have taken a shortcut and forced something to happen, but the end result would have been less than the best because it would not have been what God provided.

📖 Look at the way Jehoshaphat expressed this attitude of waiting in 2 Chronicles 20:12. Write down what you see.

_____

_____

_____

_____

Notice what Jehoshaphat acknowledges. He recognizes what he can't do, and what he doesn't know. He was facing the prospect of a war he couldn't win, and the only acceptable solution to him was for God to intervene. That is what waiting is all about. It is deciding, "I only want what God provides, no matter how long that takes." It is also an act of humility, trusting that God's ways are better than our ways.

📖 Look at the examples James presents in James 5:10–11 and record your observations.

_____

_____

_____

_____

In each and every example of the Old Testament, we see that waiting on the Lord is time well spent. The only examples of regret are those who did not wait.

While this passage makes mention of the patience of the prophets and of men like Job, the main point that relates to our consideration is the results of their endurance. James makes a pronouncement: *"We count* [them] *blessed."* In other words, in each and every example of the Old Testament, we see that waiting on the Lord is time well spent. The only examples of regret are those who didn't wait.

After months of looking, Michele and I finally said, "Lord, we aren't going to buy a house until we are sure You are the One putting it together." After that we stopped looking and fretting, and just started waiting.

After about four months, we began to see God work. A pastor friend called to let us know that a house near his had just come up for sale. It was in immaculate condition and appeared to be a good value. We were skeptical at first but my wife set up an appointment and looked at the house. As soon as she walked in the door, it felt like home to her. It was the perfect house for us, in a quiet, older neighborhood, with a large fenced-in yard and beautiful landscaping. There was a fireplace (a long-time item on my wife's wish list) and even a pool in the backyard. It was only three miles from our church and conveniently close to town. The couple selling the house had remodeled everything before they moved, including a kitchen that made my wife drool. It was everything we wanted and much more, and it was $10,000 less than anything else we had looked at! To top it off, God even threw in the down payment in the form of a surprise gift from family members. God's will was definitely worth waiting for! As we look back at what we would have been willing to settle for compared to what God provided, we know that His way is better than ours.

THE DANGER OF STRIVING

STOP SIGN
Day Four
WAITING

As we begin to get a sense of what God's will is, we are in real danger of trying to accomplish His will through our own efforts. When we put forth our own efforts, we may be tempted to take a shortcut. Satan tried to entrap Christ in the wilderness with a sinister shortcut. Satan offered Jesus all the kingdoms of the world if He would only fall down and worship him. The irony of Satan's plot is that what Satan offered Christ was indeed God's will. Christ was supposed to be King of all the earth. The key difference was that Satan tempted Christ to bypass the Cross on His way to His rightful role as King of kings.

Identify the message that Psalm 127:1 relates to this issue of waiting.

_____

_____

_____

_____

_____

_____

This verse offers a powerful motive for waiting on God. Our initiatives are meaningless and will not last if God is not in them. It doesn't mean that we can't do anything on our own, but that what we do on our own apart from God is really a waste of time. Whatever we can accomplish outside of the will of God will not be something lasting. If it isn't eternal, it is eternally insignificant.

Taking the initiative is not wrong, but we have to keep seeking God to know if He is in it or if it is all us. I really believe that God was not behind our plans to build a house. In light of our experience, consider the irony of Psalm 127:1: *"Unless the LORD builds the house, they labor in vain who build it."*

> "Unless the LORD builds the house, they labor in vain who build it; Unless the LORD guards the city, the watchman keeps awake in vain."
>
> Psalm 127:1

📖 Look at the story of Abraham in Genesis.

What was God's will for Abram (Abraham) in Genesis 15:1–6?

_____

_____

_____

_____

_____

What did Abraham do when God's will did not come to pass right away (Genesis 16:1–4)?

_____

_____

_____

_____

_____

What was the result of Abraham not waiting on the Lord (see Genesis 17–18)?

_____

_____

_____

_____

_____

Early in Abraham's journey God revealed His will to Abraham and Sarah. God was going to bless this childless family with a son. Abraham knew God's will, but he did not know how God would accomplish it. When things didn't happen right away, Abraham and Sarah took matters into their own hands. The son they had through striving (Ishmael) only produced strife. He was called *"a wild donkey of a man,"* and throughout the generations his descendants, the Arabs, have strived with Abraham's descendants, Israel. God still brought the promised son, Isaac, but there were consequences to Abraham's self-effort. They learned the hard way that it is not enough to know God's will—we must seek God's will in God's way.

Do you struggle with the temptation to cut corners? In your present situation, do you desire to take shortcuts? Perhaps you sense marriage is in your future, but because of loneliness or longing you are trying to find a mate on your timetable instead of letting God provide one on His. Or maybe you are miserable in your present job, and you realize it is not God's long-term calling for you. Are you waiting for the job God provides, or are you looking for the quickest exit from an undesirable situation?

The biggest threat to waiting is reflected in our unwillingness and in our lack of trust. If I really believe God's will is best, I should be willing to wait for it. Unwillingness to wait is a sign of a deeper problem, likely rooted in a wrong view of God. Remember, His will is always *"good, and acceptable, and perfect"* (Romans 12:2).

FOR ME TO HEAR GOD

Wait for the Lord. The call is clear. If we are to walk by faith instead of sight, we will have times of waiting. This too is God's will. Biblical waiting is not a passive response to decision making—it is faith in action. It is active trust in God and what He is able to provide. As we seek to hear God, there will be times of waiting, and we must resist the temptation to run ahead of Him and His timing.

📖 Consider the message of Isaiah 50:10–11.

What are we to do when we walk in darkness and have no light (when God is silent)?

_____

_____

_____

What wrong thing are we tempted toward (verse 11a)?

_____

_____

_____

What are the consequences of lighting our own light?

_____

_____

_____

Biblical waiting is not a passive response to decision making—it is faith in action. It is active trust in God and what He is able to provide.

In every Christian's life there will be times of darkness—times when the way is not clear and the desired light is not immediately forthcoming. When we hit those times we must trust the Lord and wait on Him. It is a matter of faith to accept that God will give us the light we need when we need it. If we don't have the light we desire, then we must rely on the Lord and wait. The temptation in such a circumstance is to produce our own light, but the consequence of such a choice is torment.

APPLY Think of a time when you failed to wait upon the Lord to shed light on a particular decision. When light from the Lord did not meet expectations or did not come according to your timetable, did you attempt to produce your own light and proceed with your initiative?

_____

_____

_____

_____

_____

_____

What were the consequences?

_____

_____

_____

_____

_____

APPLY Ask yourself the following questions as you apply this principle of waiting:

Is there any evidence that God wants me to wait on Him before resolving this decision?

What is it?

_____

_____

_____

Is there any lack of willingness on my part to wait on God?

_____

_____

_____

How would I identify it?

_____

_____

_____

What can I do while I wait?

_____

_____

_____

Maybe the most important thing you can do in your situation is the message of Psalm 46:10—*"Cease striving and know that I am God."* As you close out this week's lesson, write down a prayer of ceasing. Make it personal to your own situation.

_____

_____

_____

_____

_____

_____

_____

Notes

Notes

THE "FORK IN THE ROAD" SIGN:
The Sound Mind Principle

Sam nervously broke the lead of his pencil as he scratched meaninglessly at the project on which he was working. He'd been at it for hours but couldn't focus on what needed to be done. His mind kept leaping back to the decision looming ahead. The job offer seemed too good to be true: a $20,000 raise, his own secretary, a company car, and a job he could really sink his teeth into. At first he'd thought of it as a blessing from God, but now he wasn't so sure.

The new job would mean moving his wife and children halfway across the country, leaving their friends and family, and their church. It would uproot the kids from school, and his son Steve had just made the varsity football team. It would mean switching to a rival company. How could he tell his boss that? Fred had been more than a boss to Sam, more like the father he never had. Fred had hired Sam straight out of college and had shown him the ropes. When Sam went through a rough period just before becoming a Christian, when his drinking got out of hand, Fred had been more understanding than most bosses would have been, even keeping him on salary while he went through treatment. *How do you balance loyalty with opportunity?* Sam questioned silently.

"For God has not given us a spirit of fear, but of power and of love and of a sound mind."

2 Timothy 1:7 NKJV

His neighbor had advised him to take the job. "No one stays with the same company as long as you have anymore," the neighbor had explained. "You have to think about what is best for yourself and your family." *"But is the financial aspect the only way to measure that?"* Sam mused.

A few years ago Sam might have jumped at the opportunity. However, when he became a Christian, many things in his life changed—including his values and his dreams. He still enjoyed his work as much as ever, but now he realized that his career wasn't the only thing in his life containing meaning. His family had become a priority, and he really got a lot out of his involvement in church. Church had come to mean so much more than just biding time in the pew counting the seconds till he could hit the couch at kickoff. Now, he actually looked forward to the sermons; he even took notes, and he really liked helping out with the youth on Wednesday nights. Taking this new job would affect so much more than where he "clocked in" and to whom he answered. Beads of perspiration speckled his brow as he entreated, "What should I do, Lord?"

A few days later as we met over breakfast, Sam related his situation to me. "Eddie, how can I know what God wants me to do?" he asked in candor.

"FORK IN THE ROAD" SIGN

Day One

THE SOUND MIND PRINCIPLE

THE SOUND MIND PRINCIPLE

The last signpost we will look at on our way to finding God's will is the **FORK IN THE ROAD** sign. Life hands all of us various opportunities from time to time, and we find ourselves at a crossroad where a decision must be made. These decisions aren't always easy, though, because they have far-reaching effects. One of my favorite poems is the classic by the American poet Robert Frost, "The Road Not Taken." Drawing an allegorical picture of life, Frost uses the story of a man who encounters a fork on the path he is traveling. The concluding stanza relates,

I took the one less traveled by, and that has made all the difference.

Have you ever found yourself at a crossroad? This is where Sam found himself, and it was his first significant opportunity as a young Christian to discern God's will.

Sam edged forward in this seat with marked enthusiasm as I began relating to him the "Sound Mind Principle" of Scripture.

📖 Look at 2 Timothy 1:7.

According to this verse, what has <u>not</u> come from God?

_____

_____

_____

_____

_____

Have you ever found yourself at a crossroad?

What has come from God?

_____

_____

_____

_____

In 2 Timothy 1:7 we read, *"For God has not given us a spirit of timidity, but of power and love and discipline."* Other translations render the word "discipline" as *"a sound mind"* or *"sound judgment."* In other words, God gave us a mind that works. If we are walking with Him, we don't disengage our brain—we use it. The key is **if** we are walking with Him.

📖 In 1 Corinthians 2:14—3:3 the apostle Paul explains a concept key to the sound mind principle. Look at the passage and answer the questions that follow.

Identify the three different persons spoken of in this passage.

_____

_____

_____

_____

Who is the "we" spoken of here?

_____

_____

_____

_____

What is the difference between *"he who is spiritual"* and *"babes in Christ"*?

_____

_____

_____

_____

"We have the mind of Christ" is an interesting statement, but what does it mean? To begin with, who is the "we" spoken of here who have "the mind of Christ"? As you look back through the verse you see that the obvious answer is *"he who is spiritual."* In this significant passage Paul identifies the difference between true spirituality and what was being practiced at Corinth. The *"he who is spiritual"* is contrasted in the verses that follow with *"babes in Christ"* and fleshly-minded believers. These truths reveal that the more we mature in Christ the more we will experience "sanctified reasoning"—or reasoning energized by the Spirit of God, who indwells and directs us. The wisdom of God that I have access to through the Spirit gives me more than simply a light on logic; it shows me how to "abide in the vine" (see John 15) and use what God has provided through my relationship with Him. This mind of Christ is not available to the "natural man" or unbeliever.

> **"But he who is spiritual appraises all things, yet he himself is appraised by no man. For who has known the mind of the Lord, that he should instruct Him? But we have the mind of Christ."**
>
> **1 Corinthians 2:15–16**

THE PLACE OF THE MIND IN FOLLOWING GOD

In our pursuit of God's promptings, it is important that we recognize errors awaiting us at each of the two extremes. One error we can make is to lean too heavily on human reason so that any sense of following God is lost. The other error is to be so focused on looking for some dramatic revelation from God that we discount the wisdom of our Spirit-filled mind. We find the truth between those extremes. It is found in using the mind God gave us, while looking to Him for leading. As a child matures, he depends less on his parents' directives and leans more on their teachings. In the same way, a Christian needs to grow in his ability to make biblical decisions consistent with what God has taught in His Word, and not depend on his interpretation of some dramatic sign.

📖 Read Psalm 16:7 and write what you learn there about the mind.

_____

_____

_____

_____

In this passage we see that one of the ways God counsels us is through our mind instructing us. God created us with a mind that can think and use logic. Much like a computer program, it is only as good as the information that is fed into it, but we need to understand that to be a Christian does not mean throwing away your mind.

📖 Look at Proverbs 16:9. What does it teach about taking credit for what our minds think up?

_____

_____

_____

Proverbs is a book of wisdom. In its assorted sayings we find many nuggets of wise counsel. In this verse, Solomon seems to suggest that even when we plan our way, we can't take full credit for the outcome, for the Lord is in the background directing our steps.

God created us with minds, and He intends that we use them. Yet, there is danger in trusting too much in our own logic. One near-fatal flaw we have is our innate tendency to lean on our own understanding. I'm not saying a Christian unplugs his brain when he seeks God's will, but the admonition of Proverbs 3:5–6 makes it clear that limited, finite, human reasoning isn't adequate for all the decisions we are called to make.

📖 Read Proverbs 3:5–6 and answer the questions that follow.

What is being contrasted with trusting the Lord in these verses?

_____

_____

What do you think it means to *"lean"* on your own understanding?

_____

_____

_____

How do we *"acknowledge Him"* in all our ways?

_____

_____

_____

What is the result?

_____

_____

_____

_____

Here in Proverbs 3, we see trusting the Lord contrasted with leaning on or trusting our own understanding. The Hebrew word for lean means "to support oneself." It doesn't mean that we don't use our own understanding; rather, it says that human logic alone is not sufficient to support us. The admonition to acknowledge Him in all our ways makes it clear that in every situation life brings our way, there is a need to bring that situation to the Lord through prayer. We must lean on the Lord and ask His wisdom in all our decisions. Then He will direct our paths.

Bill Bright, in "The Paul Brown Letter," gives a significant illustration of this balance between using our minds and looking for God's leading:

> It is true that God still reveals His will to some men and women in dramatic ways, but this should be considered the exception rather than the rule. . . . Philip, the deacon, was holding a successful campaign in Samaria. The "Sound Mind Principle" would have directed him to continue his campaign. However, God overruled by a special revelation, and Philip was led by the Holy Spirit to preach Christ to the Ethiopian eunuch. According to tradition, God used the Ethiopian eunuch to communicate the message of our living Lord to his own country.

The point here is not that a Spirit-filled mind is inadequate, but that it is incomplete.

Sometimes the best laid decision based upon available information is inadequate—because the information is inadequate. Philip could see only the immediate fruit of his ministry in Samaria, but God saw the long-term fruit from the witnessing opportunity with the Ethiopian. It is easy to count the number of seeds in an apple, but only God can count the number of apples that come from one seed.

As Sam struggled with his decision, I didn't tell him to avoid searching for dramatic leadings of God, but I wanted to get him to look also at the objective facts of his decision. With a Spirit-filled mind, we can trust our reasoning to "appraise" the situation as 1 Corinthians 2:15 puts it. But how do we do that?

God created us with minds, and He intends that we use them. Yet, there is danger in trusting too much in our own logic. One near-fatal flaw we have is our innate tendency to "lean on our own understanding."

It is easy to count the number of seeds in an apple, but only God can count the number of apples that come from one seed.

To appraise the situation accurately, we need to apply the signposts we have already talked about, such as counsel **(INFORMATION SIGN)**, stewardship **(CARPOOL SIGN)**, providential circumstances **(DETOUR SIGN)**, and so on. This **FORK IN THE ROAD** or "sound mind" signpost is different in that it synthesizes all of the attributes of the first eleven signposts we have studied into a coherent, systematic form. Incidentally, this is why the **FORK IN THE ROAD** sign is the final signpost of our study.

"FORK IN THE ROAD" SIGN

Day Three

THE SOUND MIND PRINCIPLE

PUTTING THE PIECES TOGETHER

How do we use our minds without negating the spiritual dimension? One important factor is to keep our minds open. If we see God's will as a point, then as soon as we think we know His will, we close our minds to other options. But if we understand that God reveals His will in a progressive way, then we keep an open mind even when we think we know the answer.

APPLY Think about how the Bible was written.

How long did it take for the Bible to be written?

_____

_____

What does this say about God's methods of revealing wisdom to man?

_____

_____

_____

God's revelation was progressive. Adam and Eve didn't have as much information about God as Moses did. But even Moses didn't have the advantage of the New Testament and the teachings of Christ. After our Lord ascended, the Holy Spirit came, and more revelation came to the apostles. I think it is important to see this progression of God's will being revealed, especially when we consider how God reveals His will to us today.

📖 Look at Matthew 22:37. What role does the mind play in our worship of God?

_____

_____

_____

_____

"Jesus said unto him, 'Thou shalt love the Lord thy God with all thy heart, and with all thy soul, and with all thy mind.'"

Matthew 22:37

In this verse of Scripture, Jesus admonishes us to love the Lord with all our minds. It is a significant verse, for often we try to separate the intellectual from the spiritual. This is not what God desires. He who created the mind, delights in our putting it to use. Using it properly should move us to love Him more.

📖 Read Acts 7:22–23. How did Moses begin moving from the comfort zone of Pharoah's court to identifying with the people of his birth?

_____

_____

_____

_____

It is important to notice that God used Moses' mind to direct him toward his people. While the process was a long one, and Moses made some mistakes along the way, the "spiritual" leading was not against his mind but with it.

Putting the pieces together in decision-making involves important steps. To make the most of the minds God gave us, we must put them to orderly use. We must take the time to **identify** our options. We must **qualify** our options by identifying the pros and cons of each. Then we must try to **quantify** our evaluation. This is done by attaching a numeric value, a priority or level of importance, if you will, to our pros and cons. Finally we must **justify** our results, reconciling the accounts of each to determine if there is a strong leading indicator. Let's look at how this works out.

Sam and I started through this process in his decision. We walked through it step by step, first identifying his options. As we started writing, Sam identified two options: **(1)** stay where he was; or **(2)** accept the other job offer. This may sound fine, but remember our early look at the binary trap.

"One of the things to realize, Sam," I related, "is that God may have allowed this situation for reasons we don't yet see."

Sometimes it takes a decision like this to move us out of neutral. Sometimes God uses a situation to get our attention and then leads us in a different direction altogether. Without the job offer, Sam probably would not have taken the time to evaluate his career.

"I would encourage you to include at least one other column for God to fill in if He chooses," I suggested. When he had done this, I had him write a simplified statement clarifying each option.

Next we qualified his options. We wrote out the pros and cons of each option as completely as possible. We did this not as an evaluation, but as a thorough, objective consideration of each option. Determining pros and cons may require drawing on outside resources, such as the counsel of others. It took several days for Sam to complete his list. He spent hours talking it over with his wife, and he even involved the kids in making the lists. He also met with his pastor and his Sunday school teacher. He finally produced a list that satisfied him.

Then, we had to quantify his list, giving each pro and each con a number value from 1 to 5. For example, time with his family was valued at 5, being quite important. This was a "pro" on his present job, but a potential "con" on the other offer. Salary was valued at 3, not unimportant, but not all-important either. There are no standard numerical values—it depends on how important something is to the individual. Salary might be more important to others.

Quantifying Sam's list proved to be a laborious process, but nonetheless extremely worthwhile. Sam said, "It made me take the time to think about my values and to take a long look at all sides of the decision."

Our last step was to justify his columns. We added them up and subtracted the numerical value of the cons from the pros for each option. This process translates subjective values into measurable criteria. As a result, Sam was able to see more clearly how much he had in his present job. Maybe the other job offered a bigger paycheck, but that isn't the only yardstick of a career. "If all that mattered was money," Sam explained, "there wouldn't be much meaning in it."

Sam decided to stay where he was, but the process showed him why he was there, and in the end he experienced the confirming work of God's peace.

"FORK IN THE ROAD" SIGN

Day Four

THE SOUND MIND PRINCIPLE

> "It [assessing numerical values to the pros and cons of a decision] made me take the time to think about my values and to take a long look at all sides of the decision."
>
> —"Sam"

POTENTIAL PROBLEMS

Like each of the other signposts, the **FORK IN THE ROAD** sign is not immune from being misinterpreted. One of the ways we can be misled by this sign is by having too much of a "calculator mentality." The benefit of the process is not in adding and subtracting but in thoroughly thinking through the pros and cons. We may conclude that a certain course is right even if it didn't win mathematically. Remember our focus should not be on the numbers but on what we sense God is saying.

📖 Look at Matthew 16:21–23.

What is the message of Jesus that Peter is struggling with?

_____

_____

_____

What is Peter's logic telling him?

_____

_____

_____

What do we learn from Jesus' response?

_____

_____

_____

Peter must have had a hard time going from "teacher's pet" to "teacher's dog" in one quick move. He started by winning a compliment for recognizing that Jesus was the Christ (Messiah). But then a moment later he is identified as Satan and sternly rebuked by Jesus. The problem here is Peter's "calculator mentality." It just did not add up to him that Jesus would suffer or be killed. Peter's logic told him that Jesus needed to take over rather than become a human sacrifice. It is a significant point that Jesus tells Peter the problem was not his mind but where his mind was set—on man's interests instead of God's.

📖 Read 1 Corinthians 3:1–3.

What difference is there between the thinking of a "babe" in Christ and the thinking of a "natural man" (unbeliever)?

_____

_____

_____

_____

_____

The other potential danger with this signpost occurs when we aren't operating with a Spirit-filled mind. In 1 Corinthians 3, Paul indicates that the fleshly-minded believer operates in the same dimension as an unbeliever. If there is unconfessed sin in my life and I am not filled with the Holy Spirit, I cannot use the sound mind principle, for I will be "leaning on my own understanding." I do not have the "mind of Christ" unless I am one "who is spiritual."

📖 Look at Romans 8:6 in the sidebar

What is the fruit of a mind set on the flesh?

_____

_____

_____

_____

> *"For the mind set on the flesh is death, but the mind set on the Spirit is life and peace, . . ."*
>
> **Romans 8:6**

What is the fruit of a mind set on the Spirit?

_____

_____

_____

_____

If anything grabs our attention it should be this one point – focus is paramount! Where our minds are focused will determine in large part whether they help us or hinder us. The mind set on the flesh (sinful nature) brings deadness into our lives, but a mind set on the Spirit brings life—not just existence, but real life.

If you are uncertain about where you stand, invite God to bring to mind any unresolved areas of sin. Confess them to Him and repent of them, and then reaffirm your yieldedness to His reign in your life. That is the key to operating in "sanctified reasoning."

"FORK IN THE ROAD" SIGN

Day Five

THE SOUND MIND PRINCIPLE

FOR ME TO HEAR GOD

The key to the sound mind principle is being in right relationship with God. Only "he who is spiritual" can operate with the mind of Christ.

This last signpost affords you the opportunity to wrap up your decision-making process. Remember, the key to the sound mind principle is being in right relationship with God. Only "he who is spiritual" can operate with the mind of Christ. The unbeliever does not understand the things of God. Sovereign wisdom is foolishness to him. The carnal or fleshly believer may have a relationship with God because of his faith in Christ. Yet if he isn't walking in fellowship with God, he isn't able to draw on the resources of his relationship with God. He is walking like a "mere man" in human wisdom. A right relationship with God—one with yieldedness to Christ and His will and with no unconfessed sin—is the key to operating with Christ's wisdom.

 I hope that by now you have thoroughly defined your options. Take time to review these steps to the sound mind principle, and then work them out on the charts provided.

Step 1: Identify
Identify your options. Clarify as well as you can exactly what your options are. Avoid the "Binary Trap"—don't limit yourself to any either-or decisions. Make room for God to reveal something different. When you have done this, write a simplified title for each option in the spaces provided at the top of the chart.

Option A:

_____

_____

_____

_____

_____

_____

Option B:

_____

_____

_____

_____

_____

Option C: (God may have to fill this one in over time.)

_____

_____

_____

_____

_____

_____

Step 2: Qualify

List the pros and cons of each option. Don't worry yet about evaluating. Just write them down. Include also the counsel of others in these lists.

Step 3: Quantify

Wait until you have written down all the pros and cons that come to mind before you begin this step. Once your pros and cons are listed, assess the value of each of the pros according to their importance to you and to the decision. Use the numbers 1 to 5, 5 being the most important, and write that number in the value column. Quantify the value of each of the cons in the same way.

Step 4: Justify

Now total your columns and subtract the cons from the pros for each option. This doesn't mean you'll always be led to choose the winner, but the process will help you consider all your choices more thoroughly.

PRO-CON SHEET

Example: Sam's Option #1—Taking the New Job

PROS	VALUE	CONS	VALUE
More money	3	Have to move	2
Private secretary	2	Leave friends	3
Company car	2	Leave church	4
Job challenge	4	Work more hours	3
Nicer home & neighborhood	3	Further from relatives	2
Higher cost of living	1	Adjustments of kids	3
Total	14	Total	18
		Difference	-4

You have to choose to be totally honest with what is really important to you and how important it is.

As you can see, writing out the pros and cons is a subjective process that you seek to deal with in an objective way. You have to choose to be totally honest with **what** entities are really important to you and **how** important each entity is. You have to think through all the different facets of each option. The real value of this approach is that it helps you to consider your options more thoroughly because you put the different strengths and weaknesses down on paper. This process may take some time. You may think of things that require further research to determine if they are indeed pros or cons. You may have to allow some time to process these pros and cons—for example, adjustments of the kids may only be a short-term negative. The important thing is that you take the time to look as objectively as you can at each of your options and compare them against each other instead of basing your decision on shifting feelings. Why not apply this method now to your own decision-making.

OPTION #1:

PROS	VALUE	CONS	VALUE

OPTION #2:

PROS	VALUE	CONS	VALUE

OPTION #3:

PROS	VALUE	CONS	VALUE

You may find yourself returning to these lists more than once. See this as a process, not a point. It will be helpful though, if you will take the time to cement this in prayer. . . .

Dear Lord, more than anything else, I want to know Your will. I know that if my will is different than Yours, Your will is best. I trust that it is good, acceptable, and perfect. Help me to see what You are saying to me through my circumstances and the counsel of those around me. Make me sensitive to the voice of Your Spirit. Show me if there are any motives I need to lay down. Help me to face my fears and trust them to You. Protect me from a fleshly agenda. Guard my heart with your peace as I walk by faith and wait on You. Amen.

You may want to write a prayer of your own in the space below. . . .

_____

_____

_____

_____

_____

_____

_____

_____

_____

Notes

Notes

RECOGNIZING THE SIGNPOSTS:
Following God's Will

Some time ago I spent a weekend alone with my oldest son Blake. We had many chances to talk without interruption, a rarity in a family of six. Over the next several days, I saw some real progress in what had been problem areas for him. I wasn't trying to make it a teaching time; I had no hidden agenda or ulterior motives. We just hung out together. We played some board games. We ate dinner at his favorite restaurant. We went to the mall together. We just had a lot of unhurried, unharried time. As I reflect back on that weekend, I realize how we both needed it. As a father, I had been doing a good job of communicating what I desired his behavior and priorities to be, but what made the difference for him was the relationship time. That gave him the "want to" to obey.

As I reflect on the will of God, I realize how essential it is that we don't simply focus on the **rules** of our faith, but that we work to develop our **relationship** with God. If our relationship with God is healthy and in place, then finding God's will is not a separate pursuit but a natural dimension of what is already going on.

As we look back over the signposts, we need to note one point. The things we have talked about are not separate from our normal, daily walk with Christ; rather, they are the central aspects of it.

As we look back over the signposts, we need to note one point. The things we have talked about are not separate from our normal, daily walk with Christ; rather, they are the central aspects of it.

Prayer, study of the Scriptures, the ministry of the Holy Spirit, the lordship of Jesus Christ, and our stewardship are all vital dimensions of our day-to-day walk with the Lord. When we have a need for wisdom in decisions, these aspects become focused in that direction—but only if they are already there. That's when finding God's will means less drama and less trauma.

The will of God is not a hidden mystery revealed to the super-spiritual or held only for a special event. It is an integral part of what it means to walk with Christ. As we have learned, though, finding the will of God is a process. Pursuing God's will is punctuated with points, but if we look at this pursuit only in isolated instances, we miss the big picture God wants us to see. It may be that the major decisions confronting us are there to underscore what isn't there in our relationship with God. As we wrap up our study of decision-making as it relates to God's will, I'd like to isolate the key issues of **walking** in the will of God, not simply **finding** it.

God Wants You to Know His Will

It is important to remember that God really wants us to know His will. Discerning His will is not a game of hide and seek. God never hides His will. Whether or not we are able to hear Him depends on how ready we are to listen. Consider this analogy. A father watching from the window sees his young toddler who has been playing in the yard and now heads for the street. He yells to the child to stop, but the child doesn't hear. What will the father do? Will he resign himself to an attitude of, "Oh well, I told my will. It's up to the child to find it"? No way! The father will make sure he communicates his will in a way the child can hear and respond to, even if it means running outside and grabbing the child before he endangers himself. How much more will God, our heavenly Father, communicate His will to His children in a way they can understand?

Now, let's carry the analogy a step further. That same father will communicate his will a little differently to the older child or to the child who is hearing but not obeying. But the will is the same and the commitment to communicate it remains the same as well.

You Must Decide If You Want His Will

In order for us to hear what God is saying, we must be listening. We must decide we want His will, not our own. Until that issue is settled, we will make little progress in finding God's will.

Consider again the analogy of the parent-child relationship. The child who runs away from home and doesn't talk with his parents will not have access to their wisdom. So, too, if we are not in fellowship with God and walking with Him, to seek His will and wisdom in a decision puts the cart before the horse. We must first make sure our relationship with Him is right.

Of course, the analogy breaks down if you carry it too far. God our heavenly Father gives grace in ways no human parent ever could.

Discerning His will is not a game of hide and seek. God never hides His will.

THE PIVOTAL ISSUE OF JESUS' LORDSHIP

As I talk with people everywhere—in America, in Eastern Europe, in the Caribbean, wherever—I find that most Christians struggle with God's will at one basic point. More of a problem than our finding God's will is our settling that God's will is what we want. I have a will also. And when God's will and my will don't match, a decision must be made. I must answer the question: Who is Lord of this area of my life? It doesn't matter what I sing, what I profess, or what I believe intellectually. If I choose my will over God's, then in this area Christ is not Lord—self is. What I have seen as I counsel Christians everywhere is that choosing to do God's will trips people up far more frequently than an inability to find it, and that is where I struggle also. What about you?

GOD'S WILL AND GOD'S NATURE

Romans 12:2 is one verse of Scripture that has helped me choose God's will even when I fail to understand how it fits with what I want. In that verse we are told that turning from the world and cultivating a renewed mind via the Scriptures give me opportunities to *"prove what the will of God is, that which is good, and acceptable, and perfect."* As I look back over my Christian experience, I can honestly say I have never regretted doing the will of God. It has always been good in the end. I have, however, regretted doing the will of self. Every time I choose God's will, I prove to myself and to all who see that the will of God really is *"good, and acceptable, and perfect."* I have never seen it not be.

The will of God in any situation will always be exactly as the Bible describes it: *"good, and acceptable, and perfect."* It always offers more than my will offers. It always fulfills me than my will does. It will always, in the end, satisfy me in a way that my will never could. God's will is better for me than my own because of His very nature. He is good. If I struggle with the will of God, I am really struggling with the nature of God. It is no small wonder that the first appearance of sin in human history originated when Eve, through Satan's prompting, questioned the goodness of the will of God. Do I really believe that God is good? If He is, then so is His will. If I turn from God's will, I turn to a lie.

An incident in Peter's life described in John 6 continually ministers to me. Peter and other followers of Christ had reached a crossroad in their involvement with Christ's earthly ministry. (Remember the Fork in the Road signpost?) Many of those who had been following Christ had withdrawn from Him, as His teaching and expectations became too demanding for them. Verse 67 records that Jesus leaned over to His chosen disciples (the Twelve) and said, *"You do not want to go away also, do you?"*

Simon Peter pipes up in the very next verse and says, *"Lord, to whom shall we go? You have words of eternal life."* In essence Peter is saying, "Lord, if I turn from You, I am turning to a lie." When I struggle with what I sense God is saying, I am reminded that He alone is truth. If I turn from Him, I turn to a lie.

What I have seen in my own heart is that once Christ's lordship of an area is settled, the will of God in this area is demystified. In other words, His will isn't so difficult to grasp anymore. What I hope you discover as you deal

> As I counsel Christians everywhere I have seen that choosing to do God's will trips people up far more frequently than finding it, and that is where I struggle also. What about you?

> What I hope you discover as you deal with your own decisions is that God's will really is "good, and acceptable, and perfect."

> *You will not discover how good God's will is until you choose to follow it.*

with your own decisions is that God's will really is "good, and acceptable, and perfect." Yet, you will not discover how good God's will is until you choose to follow it. When you do choose the will of God, you will experience what you already know, the goodness of God and His will.

As you make choices that reflect God's will, others will be encouraged when they see the goodness of God's will manifested in your life, and unbelievers will see in you the attractiveness of Christianity.

My prayer for you is that you would know the joy of walking in the will of God, moment by moment! I hope this book proves helpful to you in that process.

PART ONE

God's Will and Your Life Mate

Some who purchase this book will do so because they are trying to determine God's will concerning engagement and marriage. Perhaps you find yourself in these shoes. If you do, let me share with you some principles that are particularly relevant to the life-mate decision. You will be encouraged to know that for most of us, marriage will be God's will. But the other side of the coin is that singleness is God's will for all of us! Now, for most of us that singleness will not last a lifetime, but it is essential that we realize that singleness is not waiting for the will of God—rather, it is part of it.

Not Finding but Becoming

I think one of the biggest mistakes a Christian can make is to put all the emphasis on "finding 'the' one." You see, since singleness is, at least for a time, God's will for every one of us, then He can and does use it for our good. I do not believe we will find "the one" until we become who God wants us to be. This means learning lessons from singleness. When we *become* the right mate, then we are free to *find* the right mate.

What is the primary lesson of singleness? Is it self-control? Is it personal maturity? Is it patience? If your singleness is as mine was,

I think one of the biggest mistakes a Christian can make is to put all the emphasis on "finding 'the' one."

you may see that the primary lesson is, you don't like being single. But there is a far more important lesson that many people miss. In fact, I believe missing this is at the root of many problems that can arise after marriage. In 1 Corinthians 7, the apostle Paul talks much about marriage and singleness, and in verse 35 he gives what I believe to be the primary purpose for our singleness: *"to secure undistracted devotion to the Lord."* Before we can handle the responsibilities of married life, we must first learn what it means for Christ to be preeminent. Of course, we never stop learning that lesson, but if Christ is not made preeminent when we are still single, it will be much harder to make Him preeminent when we are married.

Marriage is great, a tremendous blessing; it is a beautiful thing. I am so grateful for the godly wife I am blessed with and for the many ways God uses her in my life. But marriage isn't everything. It was never intended to be. Many couples are disillusioned because they enter matrimony with the expectation that their wife or husband is going to meet all their needs, and when it doesn't happen, they are disappointed. But God never intended our mate to be saddled with so great a responsibility. The only one capable of meeting all our needs is God. He can meet some of those needs through our mate if He chooses, but ultimately He is the one we must look to for sustenance.

Let me illustrate what I mean. Take my desire for intimacy. If I expect my mate to meet that need and she doesn't, it will move me to sulk, or become angry, or demand more than she can deliver. If I look to God to meet that need through my mate, and she doesn't meet it, that will move me to prayer, to self-examination, and to asking God what He wants me to see. He may be using that area to get my attention and to teach me something or to reveal a particular area of my life He wants to deal with.

You see, God must be at the core of our lives. Putting Him there is, I believe, the primary purpose for our singleness. It is an opportunity for **undistracted devotion** (see sidebar note) which then serves as the foundation for every other lesson we must learn—in singleness and in marriage, indeed in all of life. Once that undistracted devotion to the Lord is secured, then we are able to enter into marriage as we should. Our relationship with God gives us the ability to give what we should in a marriage relationship.

MAKING THE DECISION

As with any area of decision making, if I am not careful in my choice of a life mate, I can err in one of two extremes: **(1)** by seeing the decision as solely mine and not seeking God's wisdom at all; or **(2)** by being so focused on finding "the one" God has selected that I don't take any responsibility for the decision myself. Proper decision making lies somewhere between the two extremes.

Is there only one person I can marry? I don't pretend to know the answer to that complex question. I do know, however, that God's Word limits who I can marry, and that He has unlimited wisdom for every decision I must make. Certainly, He is in the middle of so important a decision as this, and we must seek His will.

I believe that all the principles we have discussed in this book come into play in the choice of a life mate. Lordship must be settled. We must pray, search the Scriptures, obtain counsel and count the cost. Marriage is a decision to

---

UNDISTRACTED DEVOTION

In 1 Corinthians 7, Paul offers guidelines for marriage, divorce, and for those who are single. Paul considered it ideal for a Christian to remain single:

"But I want you to be free from concern. One who is unmarried is concerned about the things of the Lord, how he may please the Lord; but one who is married is concerned about the things of the world, how he may please his wife, and his interests are divided. And the woman who is unmarried, and the virgin, is concerned about the things of the Lord, that she may be holy both in body and spirit; but one who is married is concerned about the things of the world, how she may please her husband. And this I say for your own benefit; not to put a restraint upon you, but to promote what is seemly, and to secure undistracted devotion to the Lord." (1 Corinthians 7:32–35)

take seriously! But we must realize that, especially in this arena, decision-making involves more than just gathering information or interpreting emotions. It also involves the will—I must make the choice to surrender my singleness and its freedoms, and to commit myself permanently to another person for her betterment and not simply mine.

If, after going through the process discussed in this book, you still have problems making the decision, let me share with you some helpful principles. They come from a seminar called "God's Will for Marriage," a special engaged couple's part of the Family Life Conference, "A Weekend To Remember" sponsored by the Family Ministry. I strongly encourage all engaged couples and those contemplating marriage to attend one of these weekends. It will be an invaluable investment in your married life. My wife and I attended one about six months before we were married and were ministered to so much that we have gone back four times as a married couple. For information on the dates of conferences near you, write or call:

The Family Ministry
P.O. Box 23840
Little Rock, AR 72221-3840
Phone 501/223-8663

The following information on "getting off the fence" is from pages 57–59 of the Family Life Conference notebook and has been reprinted by permission.

GETTING OFF THE FENCE

Have you been "on the fence" for a period of time in making this decision? Have you been dating for "forty years" but just aren't quite sure if this is God's "one" for you? You may be lingering in your decision for one of several reasons:

(1) You may have a personal history of indecisiveness. Perhaps you grew up in a home where your decisions were always criticized by your parents and you have trouble trusting your decisions.

(2) Another reason might be that pain from past relationships or failed relationships around you causes you to fear making a commitment.

(3) A third reason for your indecisiveness could be that God is leading the two of you apart.

If you have been on the fence for too long, each of you should get alone with God for forty-eight hours to help confirm His will. The following steps are suggested guidelines for this process:

STEP #1: Ask yourself if you are right with God. Confess your sins and humble yourself before Him. Relinquish all rights to your life to your heavenly Father.

STEP #2: List your fears.

STEP #3: Confess or acknowledge them to God.

Have you been on the fence for a period of time in making a decision concerning marriage?

STEP #4: Commit to God to accept or reject the other person as God's provision for your needs.

STEP #5: Write out that commitment to God.

STEP #6: Hold your decision privately for twenty-four hours, allowing God to confirm it with His peace.

STEP #7: Tell one close friend. This allows him or her to confirm your decision and to hold you accountable.

STEP #8: Verbalize your decision to your potential mate.

After the decision has been made, it is important to protect yourself (and your potential mate) from backing down on your commitment. Once God has directed you, procrastination can lead you back to indecisiveness. So verbalize your commitment! If you decide it is not God's will for you to marry, it is essential that you make a clean break. The Family Life ministry strongly suggests that there be no communication between the two of you for six months. If it seems that God is leading the relationship back together, then wise counsel should be sought before re-establishing contact. Perhaps the close friend you confided in is a good person to start with.

And remember, God's will is ultimately known by faith. *"Without faith it is impossible to please Him, for he who comes to God must believe that He is, and that He is the rewarder of those who seek Him"* (Hebrews 11:6).

If you decide it is God's will for the two of you to marry, it is important to protect yourself from doubts. Bring doubts out into the open, discuss them, and deal with them as they arise. Become accountable to others for your decision. This will help. If either one of you is totally overwhelmed with doubts that he or she cannot control and the Lord does not remove them, the only option is to break the relationship. A broken relationship is better than a broken marriage.

If you decide it is not God's will for the two of you to marry, it is essential that you make a clean break. . . .

. . . If you decide it is God's will for the two of you to marry, it is important to protect yourself from doubts.

God's Will and Career Choices

Some who purchase this book will do so because they are trying to determine God's will concerning a career choice or change. Perhaps you find yourself in these shoes. If you do, let me share with you some principles that are particularly relevant to career decisions. You will be encouraged to know that God's Word has quite a bit to say about our vocations.

Contrary to what you may have been taught, work did not originate after the fall. Work was part of God's design from the beginning. Adam began his stay in Eden with a job description. He was assigned the managerial post of "CEO of Creation." In Genesis 1:28 we read that he and Eve were responsible to *"rule over...every living thing that moves on the earth."* In chapter 2 we see this expanded. Verse 15 tells us that God *"took man and put him in the garden to cultivate it and keep it."* We also see Adam with the responsibility and authority to name all the animals God created. All of this is before sin ever became an issue. After the fall, sweat enters the picture—but work is not punishment. It is holy and meaningful.

In John 4:34 Jesus tells us, *"My food is to do the will of Him who sent Me."* I don't want to stretch the meaning of this verse

You should be encouraged to know that God's Word has quite a bit to say about our vocations.

further than it goes, but think a moment about the purpose of food. Food sustains us and satisfies us. God put the flavor in food; man didn't. I think it is legitimate to say that God's plan for our lives will both sustain us and satisfy us.

FINDING A LIFE PURPOSE

Maybe all you are trying to figure out right now is whether to say yes or no to a job opportunity. Or perhaps you are dissatisfied where you are, and you want God to provide something else. Or you might be about to graduate from college and begin interviewing. Maybe you are in college, or headed that way, and are trying to settle on a major field of study. If you want long-term answers, it is important that you look beyond your immediate situation. In order to know what job to take or what field to major in, you need to have a general sense of the career which God has called you. And to have that sense, you need to go a little further and develop a life purpose. Unfortunately, many people I meet have no real sense of any life purpose. They see the only reason for having a job as being able to pay the bills. There will be little satisfaction if the only return you get from your career is money.

But how does one go about getting a sense of life purpose? First of all, the whole counsel of God's Word indicates that there is much more to life purpose than fulfillment of self. In the upper room, Jesus prayed, *"I have glorified Thee on the earth, having accomplished the work which Thou hast given Me to do"* (John 17:4). This statement reveals two important dimensions of life purpose. One overriding purpose for all believers is that God would be glorified in their lives. *The Westminster Catechism* expresses it this way: "The chief aim of man is to glorify God, and to enjoy Him forever." Glorifying God involves not just our work, but every dimension of our lives. Christ clarifies, however, that one of the ways we bring glory to God is by accomplishing the work He gives us to do individually. Our vocation is part of that.

ARE YOU CALLED?

There is an erroneous idea floating around in Christendom that needs to be addressed. I meet many sincere believers who talk about "calling." They take that term from the references Paul and others make to being "called" to a certain ministry. The problem is, many people wrongly believe that if you aren't called to the ministry, then God does not care what you do with your life.

Nothing could be further from the truth.

I believe you need just as much a calling from God to be a doctor or lawyer, butcher or baker as you do to be a pastor or evangelist or missionary. Too many people use the lack of lightning from heaven or writing in the sky as an excuse to live as they want with no thought for what pleases God. Or they muddle along feeling insignificant because they aren't a part of God's elite. I believe God wants Christian doctors, Christian lawyers, Christian government officials, Christian businessmen and bosses just as much as He wants pastors and missionaries. Everything I read in Scripture prompts me to conclude that each believer is unique, precious, and significant in the plan of God, not simply those in His direct employment. To suggest otherwise is contrary to Paul's teaching in 1 Corinthians 12 which shows us the necessity of every person's contribution.

Many people wrongly believe that if you aren't "called to the ministry" then God does not care what you do with your life. Nothing could be further from the truth!

Defining Our Diversity: Spiritual Gifts

Scripture is not silent about our diversity in the body of Christ. In fact, it shows quite clearly that diversity is God's design. Every believer is endowed with at least one dimension of spiritual giftedness, and I join many others in the belief that we hold several.

As we address the issue of life purpose, we must also address this issue of spiritual giftedness. Because all believers have at least one gift, and none of us possesses them all, spiritual giftedness helps us define what our life purpose is and what it is not. Personally, I have scratched administration off my list for life purpose. I learned early in life that I possessed little ability in this area. But as one holding an "equipping" gift (teaching), I also knew that, whether as my vocation or avocation, I was destined for some form of church leadership.

Let me explain what I mean by "equipping" gifts. In Ephesians 4:11–12 we read: *"And He gave some as apostles, and some as prophets, and some as evangelist, and some as pastors and teachers,* **for the equipping of the saints** *for the work of service"* (emphasis mine).

In this passage, Christ separates five areas of giftedness and defines them as having been "given" to the church. The people in those areas of church leadership are put there to help prepare those in all other areas of giftedness for a useful place in God's plan. This helped point me in a focused direction of life purpose.

What is your area of giftedness? Knowing that will be a great help in finding where you fit. Although, from time to time, God may call you to make contributions outside your primary giftedness, your over-arching life purpose will lie in that direction, and there you will find fulfillment.

Conversely, if your vocation is not consistent with your giftedness, you will always have a nagging sense of frustration and incompleteness, no matter how much success you see.

Bringing It Into Focus

By now you may be asking, "So how do I bring my life purpose into focus?" First, you must realize that this is a time-intensive process. It will take decades to culminate. Although mine has much more focus now than when I graduated from college, I am still in the process of learning, still preparing, still growing. Fulfilling my purpose now is enlarging me for what awaits me. As I am faithful now, I lay a foundation on which to build for the future. The key is not simply finding the right place, but becoming the right person. God's number one job with me is not changing my circumstances, but changing my character.

There are several keys to clarifying life purpose. First, we must bloom where we are planted. We must learn the lessons, accomplish the tasks and fulfill the responsibilities of the present before we are ready for the future. If you aren't careful, you may become so future-focused that you miss the purpose for the present in getting you there. Second, life purpose is received, not achieved. God must open the doors for us. We must be faithful and dependent on Him to provide the opportunities. Third, life purpose is a

> *"And He gave some as apostles, and some as prophets, and some as evangelists, and some as pastors and teachers, for the equipping of the saints for the work of service, to the building up of the body of Christ. . . ."*
>
> Ephesians 4:11–12

process, not a point. The early steps I take in that direction will be pretty general. Later, those steps will become increasingly specific.

Bring on the Brass Tacks

Let's get specific and practical. How do you get from where you are to where we are talking about? First, **realize that your most significant contributions to life may be decades away!** Don't get in too big a hurry. As Miles Stanford put it in his book, *The Green Letters* (Zondervan, 1975), "When God wants to make a squash, He takes six months; when He wants to make an oak tree, He takes a hundred years."

Second, **don't bail out of where you are without a clear sense of where you are going.** Don't discard your education or present job just because things are tough. My advice is: Never simply leave something. Always be going *to* something. Don't leave your present job or place without a clear sense of God leading you to something else. If God wants you to leave, He is opening up something else for you. If you are the one wanting to leave, it may be simply because things are tough and your flesh doesn't like it. Don't make a rash, emotional decision to quit your job. Make sure that is what God is saying.

A third principle to keep things practical is this: **If you aren't satisfied, start praying and looking.** If we are walking with God, He can and does lead us through our desires. This principle doesn't contradict the previous one, but complements and balances it. There is nothing wrong with seeking God in our dissatisfaction—He may be using it to get our attention. But don't let that get you moving ahead of God. You must wait for His timing and His provision.

A fourth aspect of developing a life purpose is dialogue. **Talk long and hard** with your spouse and parents or pastor or boss **about what is important to you and how you are motivated.** God's calling is usually accompanied by a "want to" in us. We are motivated to do what we were designed to do.

What Matters in Eternity

Finally, **hold your life purpose against the backdrop of eternity.** If your life purpose does not count in eternity, then it will be eternally insignificant. Regardless of how much money you make at what you do, if there is no eternal dimension, you are headed for a midlife crisis. At some point, your goals will be reached, but you will still be dissatisfied. The most frustrated person is not the one who fails to reach his goals, but the one who reaches them and then realizes they are the wrong ones. As one man put it, "I climbed the ladder of success only to discover it was leaning against the wrong wall."

How do we evaluate things eternally? Some would say if it doesn't have to do with God's Word or men's souls, it isn't eternal. But what in the Christian life doesn't have to do with such things? If I am serious about my relationship with God, His Word ought to be impacting my business practices. The Bible ought to affect how I relate with my coworkers, my boss, or my employees. God's Word working in my life ought to affect the quality of my job performance. Do I only witness door-to-door, or do I also witness in the stands I take with clients, in the service I give customers, in the quality of the job I do?

> "When God wants to make a squash, He takes six months; when He wants to make an oak tree, He takes a hundred years."
>
> —Miles Stanford

For too long we have defined spirituality so narrowly that many see no spiritual significance in secular things. I am convinced that the line between secular and sacred is drawn not simply by what we do, but by how and why we do it. Conversely, the current epidemic of mediocrity is at least in part a result of defining that which is sacred in narrow, unbiblical terms. God can be glorified in the smallest task if it is done with His glory in view. Recently I picked up a book by Doug Sherman and William Hendricks entitled, *Your Work Matters to God* (NavPress, 1987). I was intrigued by its title because I don't think most Christians really believe what it says. It's true, though—our work really does matter to God, and we should involve Him in work-related decisions.

Notes

How to Follow God

STARTING THE JOURNEY

Did you know that you have been on God's heart and mind for a long, long time? Even before time existed you were on His mind. He has always wanted you to know Him in a personal, purposeful relationship. He has a purpose for your life and it is founded upon His great love for you. You can be assured it is a good purpose and it lasts forever. Our time on this earth is only the beginning. God has a grand design that goes back into eternity past and reaches into eternity future. What is that design?

The Scriptures are clear about God's design for man—God created man to live and walk in oneness with Himself. Oneness with God means being in a relationship that is totally unselfish, totally satisfying, totally secure, righteous and pure in every way. That's what we were created for. If we walked in that kind of relationship with God we would glorify Him and bring pleasure to Him. Life would be right! Man was meant to live that way—pleasing to God and glorifying Him (giving a true estimate of who God is). Adam sinned and shattered his oneness with God. Ever since, man has come short of the glory of God: man does not and cannot please God or give a true estimate of God. Life is not right until a person is right with God. That is very clear as we look at the many people who walked across the pages of Scripture, both Old and New Testaments.

JESUS CHRIST came as the solution for this dilemma. Jesus Christ is the glory of God—the true estimate of who God is in every way. He pleased His Father in everything He did and said, and He came to restore oneness with God. He came to give man His power and grace to walk in oneness with God, to follow Him day by day enjoying the relationship for which he was created. In the process, man could begin to present a true picture of Who God is and experience knowing Him personally. You may be asking, "How do these facts impact my life today? How does this become real to me now? How can I begin the journey of following God in this way?" To come to know God personally means you must choose to receive Jesus Christ as your personal Savior and Lord.

- First of all, you must admit that you have sinned, that you are not walking in oneness with God, not pleasing Him or glorifying Him in your life (Romans 3:23; 6:23; 8:5–8).

- It means repenting of that sin—changing your mind, turning to God and turning away from sin—and by faith receiving His forgiveness based on His death on the Cross for you (Romans 3:21–26; 1 Peter 3:18).

- It means opening your life to receive Him as your living, resurrected Lord and Savior (John 1:12). He has promised to come and indwell you by His Spirit and live in you as the Savior and Master of your life (John 14:16-21; Romans 14:7–9).

- He wants to live His life through you—conforming you to His image, bearing His fruit through you and giving you power to reign in life (John 15:1,4–8; Romans 5:17; 7:4; 8:29, 37).

You can come to Him now. In your own words, simply tell Him you want to know Him personally and you willingly repent of your sin and receive His forgiveness and His life. Tell Him you want to follow Him forever (Romans 10:9–10, 13). Welcome to the Family of God and to the greatest journey of all!!!

WALKING ON THE JOURNEY

How do we follow Him day by day? Remember, Christ has given those who believe in Him everything pertaining to life and godliness, so that we no longer have to be slaves to our "flesh" and its corruption (2 Peter 1:3-4). Day by day He wants to empower us to live a life of love and joy, pleasing to Him and rewarding to us. That's why Ephesians 5:18 tells us to *"be filled with the Spirit"*—keep on being controlled by the Spirit who lives in you. He knows exactly what we need each day and we can trust Him to lead us (Proverbs 3:5–6). So how can we cooperate with Him in this journey together?

To walk with Him *day by day* means ...

- reading and listening to His Word day by day (Luke 10:39, 42; Colossians 3:16; Psalm 19:7–14; 119:9).

- spending time talking to Him in prayer (Philippians 4:6–7).

- realizing that God is God and you are not, and the role that means He has in your life.

This allows Him to work through your life as you fellowship, worship, pray and learn with other believers (Acts 2:42), and serve in the good works He has prepared for us to do—telling others who Jesus is and what His Word says, teaching and encouraging others, giving to help meet needs, helping others, etc. (Ephesians 2:10).

God's goal for each of us is that we be conformed to the image of His Son, Jesus Christ (Romans 8:29). But none of us will reach that goal of perfection until we are with Him in Heaven, for then "we shall be like Him, because we shall see Him just as He is" (1 John 3:2). For now, He wants us to follow

Him faithfully, learning more each day. Every turn in the road, every trial and every blessing, is designed to bring us to a new depth of surrender to the Lord and His ways. He not only wants us to do His will, He desires that we surrender to His will His way. That takes trust—trust in His character, His plan and His goals (Proverbs 3:5–6).

As you continue this journey, and perhaps you've been following Him for a while, you must continue to listen carefully and follow closely. We never graduate from that. That sensitivity to God takes moment-by-moment surrender, dying to the impulses of our flesh to go our own way, saying no to the temptations of Satan to doubt God and His Word, and refusing the lures of the world to be unfaithful to the Lord who gave His life for us.

God desires that each of us come to maturity as sons and daughters: to that point where we are fully satisfied in Him and His ways, fully secure in His sovereign love, and walking in the full measure of His purity and holiness. If we are to clearly present the image of Christ for all to see, it will take daily surrender and daily seeking to follow Him wherever He leads, however He gets there (Luke 9:23–25). It's a faithful walk of trust through time into eternity. And it is worth everything. Trust Him. Listen carefully. Follow closely.

The *Following God*
Bible Character Study Series

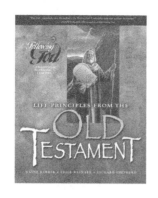

Life Principles from the Old Testament

Characters include: Adam, Noah, Job, Abraham, Lot, Jacob, Joseph, Moses, Caleb, Joshua, Gideon, and Samson
ISBN 0-89957-300-2   208 pages

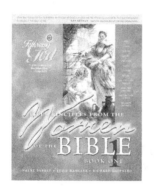

Life Principles from the Women of the Bible Book One

Characters include: Eve, Sarah, Miriam, Rahab, Deborah, Ruth, Hannah, Esther, The Virtuous Woman, Mary & Martha, Mary, the Mother of Jesus, and "The Bride of Christ."
ISBN 0-89957-302-9   224 pages.

Life Principles from the Women of the Bible Book Two

Characters include: Hagar, Lot's Wife, Rebekah, Leah, Rachel, Abigail, Bathsheba, Jezebel, Elizabeth, The Woman at the Well, Women of the Gospels, The Submissive Wife.
ISBN 0-89957-308-8   224 pages

Leaders guides also available. To order now, call (800) 266-4977 or (423) 894-6060 or visit AMGPublishers.com

The *Following God*
Bible Character Study Series

Life Principles from the Prophets of the Old Testament

Characters include: Samuel, Elijah, Elisha, Jonah, Hosea, Isaiah, Micah, Jeremiah, Habakkuk, Daniel, Haggai, and "Christ the Prophet."
ISBN 0-89957-303-7   224 pages

Life Principles from the New Testament Men of Faith

Characters include: John the Baptist, Peter, John, Thomas, James, Barnabas, Paul, Paul's Companions, Timothy, and "The Son of Man."
ISBN 0-89957-304-5   208 pages

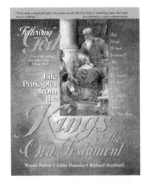

Life Principles from the Kings of the Old Testament

Characters include: Saul, David, Solomon, Jereboam I, Asa, Ahab, Jehoshaphat, Hezekiah, Josiah, Zerubbabel & Ezra, Nehemiah, and "The True King in Israel."
ISBN 0-89957-301-0   256 pages

Leaders guides also available. To order now, call (800) 266-4977 or (423) 894-6060 or visit AMGPublishers.com

Also from AMG Publishers

Life Principles for Worship from the Tabernacle

ISBN 0-89957-299-5

This Bible study is designed in an interactive format, incorporating important scriptural points of interest and will help you understand all that God says to us through the components found in Israel's Tabernacle. Important historical and symbolic details will leap from the pages and into your heart. Inside the pages you'll also find the special helps sections you've come to rely on from the best-selling "Following God" series; Word Studies, Doctrinal Notes, Did You Know?, and Stop and Apply. Each help section will add to your understanding and ability to share these new-found truths with those you know and/or teach.

In the pages of this "Following God" study on the Tabernacle you'll learn to:

- ✓ Focus on the fence, the gate and the outer court with the bronze altar and bronze laver;
- ✓ Focus on the Holy Place with the golden lamp stand, the table of showbread, and the altar of incense;
- ✓ Move into the Holy of Holies through the veil, and look at the ark of the covenant with the golden jar of manna, Aaron's rod that budded, the tables of the covenant, the mercy seat and, ultimately, the cloud of glory.

Most importantly, you'll discover how God has provided a way for man to draw near to Him.

To order, call (800) 266-4977 or (423) 894-6060.

Notes

Notes

Notes

Notes

56651902R00117